Conceiving in the Heart

stories of love and adoption

Compiled By

Deana Coreen Kastello

Conceiving in the Heart

stories of love and adoption

Deana Coreen Kastello

CFI
Springville, Utah

© 2009 Deana Coreen Kastello

All rights reserved.

No part of this book may be reproduced in any form whatsoever, whether by graphic, visual, electronic, film, microfilm, tape recording, or any other means, without prior written permission of the publisher, except in the case of brief passages embodied in critical reviews and articles.

This is not an official publication of The Church of Jesus Christ of Latter-day Saints. The opinions and views expressed herein belong solely to the author and do not necessarily represent the opinions or views of Cedar Fort, Inc. Permission for the use of sources, graphics, and photos is also solely the responsibility of the author.

ISBN 13: 978-1-59955-262-0

Published by CFI, an imprint of Cedar Fort, Inc., 2373 W. 700 S., Springville, UT 84663
Distributed by Cedar Fort, Inc., www.cedarfort.com

LIBRARY OF CONGRESS CATALOGING-IN-PUBLICATION DATA

Kastello, Deana Coreen.
  Conceiving in the heart / Deana Coreen Kastello.
    p. cm.
  Summary: Collection of stories about the children who were in the author's foster care, with discussion of adoption.
  ISBN 978-1-59955-262-0
  1. Foster children—Anecdotes. 2. Foster home care—Anecdotes. 3. Adoption. I. Title.

  HV875.K356 2009
  362.73'3—dc22

                    2009002829

Cover design by Angela D. Olsen
Cover design © 2009 by Lyle Mortimer
Edited and typeset by Heidi Doxey

Printed in the United States of America

10 9 8 7 6 5 4 3 2 1

Printed on acid-free paper

I dedicate this book to my husband, Andrew,
and our amazing, beautiful children:
Daniel, Elahanna, Noah, Halle, Saraya, and Ammon.
Without them my life would be empty and meaningless.

During the publication of this book we were richly blessed once more through the miracle of adoption. Our sixth child arrived in January 2009. There were a number of unusual events leading us to him, which showed us once more the Lord's powerful hand in our lives.

Once again his ways were certainly not ours, and thank goodness for that. How grateful we are for the tender mercies of the Lord, but mostly, his great love.

United together in voice, everyone who has shared their story in this book has done so purely out of love and commitment to the thousands of children longing for a family. I thank them.

May God continue to unite families together.

Contents

Preface ix
Our Journey 1
    Benjamin 4
        Ben's Story 7
    Daniel 11
    Elahanna 13
    Noah Michael 17
    Halle Joan 19
    Saraya 23
    Conceiving in the Heart 25

The Life of Gabrielle 27
Dear Birth Parent 31
From My Arms to Yours 37
The Phone Finally Rang! 41
Rainbows 45
My Sweet M&M 53
Love Is Love! 56
Our Road to Adoption 58
My Tracey 70
Beautiful Angels 73
Sasha 77
His Sweet Little Face 81
MY Michael 83
Abounding Joy 88

$200 in Pregnancy Tests!..................................... 91
By the Grace of God 98
    Thank You, Mom 100
A Potluck Brought Us Five Little Ducks 101
Our Infertility/Adoption Experiences........................ 106
Still Honeymooning!... 109
Mallory 113
Busy, Noisy, and Very Happy..................................117
A Mother's Perspective......................................121
What God Has Joined Together............................... 126
Heaven Sent Four 136
A Sister's Prayer 141
A Reason to Celebrate 144
MY Destinee 150
Adoption—It's All About Love 153
From Russia to China 156
Henry and Jack and a Mommy Makes Three................... 164
Nicole 170
When All the No's Finally Become Yes!........................172
Bringing Our Children Home................................. 178
I Had Dreamed of Being a Mother 186
You're Never Too Old to Make a Difference!...................189

Preface

After playing religiously with my dolls until age fourteen, I knew it was my deepest desire to be a mother. Fourteen years later, being married and trying desperately to conceive a child without any luck was not something I had planned for. I spent many countless hours on my knees, praying for a miracle.

The pain of infertility was like an emotional roller-coaster ride that I could never get off. It was a nightmare. Through our journey of infertility, God was finally able to work with me and my husband, Andrew, to open our hearts to other options. Even though my desire to conceive had always been there, receiving our first child truly changed our lives and our hearts. The many stories contained in this book are told by real people who are great examples of how being an adoptive or foster parent can be a life-changing and wonderful experience.

This book is meant to help send a positive word to all those longing to have a family. The voices of all these selfless, kind-hearted, devoted people, who have opened their hearts and taken the giant leap of faith into the unknown world of adoption and foster care, should be a comfort to those who want to make a life-changing difference to a child. Their voices are far-reaching and are here to sound the call to serve those who are in need of a family.

We are living in a day when there are far too many children born exposed or addicted to drugs, when too many children are starving, abandoned, abused, or severely neglected. The need for loving parents is a global one. The need in our own country is shocking, considering we live in the most abundant nation in the world. There are thousands of children in foster homes in the United States. In my home state of Michigan alone there are currently 19,071 children in need of a home. Agencies in every state are desperately trying to raise awareness of the continuous need for families that exists in our own backyard.

These children come in all ages, sizes, and colors. Teenagers need and deserve love, a home and a family, as do infants, toddlers, and older children. The need is *great*. Please, if you are touched in any way by the stories in this book, reach down inside yourself and find that seed of love. Don't just put these stories down feeling relief that there are amazing, giving people out there. It's true that there are many people such as those who are in this book that are changing the lives of children. But there are just not enough. Be one of those people that you admire. You too can make a difference. "I didn't say it would be easy, I just said it would be worth it."

Remember it is our children who hold the keys to our future. Let's help them be the beautiful healthy people they are destined to be. They need *us*, but we also need *them*!

Our Journey

I was twenty-five years old when I married Andrew. I thought that when I wanted to have a baby it would just happen. Pregnancy seemed like a piece of cake for everyone else, so I assumed it would be that way for me, especially as there were no health problems or issues with my female cycle. As year after year went by, I thought it odd that we had not become pregnant since we were not using any type of birth control.

All of a sudden the desire and reality of wanting a child hit me a like a great big hammer! Over the course of the next two years the despair when my period would start each month was like nothing I had ever felt before. Sex became mechanical, strained, and unenjoyable. The minute I would see or experience ovulation signs I would call my husband and demand his presence. I tried every maneuver I could find: lying on pillows, herbs, vitamins, reflexology, and even standing head-first over the bed so sperm could surely reach an egg!

Church became a chore—a nightmare actually. Big happy families and glowing pregnant women became a knife in my heart. I could no longer attend baby showers or be joyful in a friend's miracle of conception. All of these things were reminders of what I didn't have.

Finally, we sought the help of specialists to figure out the cause of our infertility. My husband, whose only transportation at that time was a bicycle eight miles one-way to work, had to deliver his "sample" within thirty minutes after stopping at a grocery store bathroom for the embarrassing event.

Desperately trying to find the cause of my infertility, I endured Clomed, shots, ultrasound tests, and uncomfortable procedures at the doctor's office and hospital. My efforts literally consumed every thought and feeling. Many tears were shed during this difficult period.

Why, God? I would ask. It seemed so unfair that there were many women whom I knew that became mothers even though they didn't necessarily want to! It seemed as though they could bring life into the world just by looking at a pair of pants. I knew I would be a great mother, nurturing and kind. I was obsessed with these feelings to the point that I was surprised at where my thoughts sometimes led me.

One of these scary thoughts occurred when I was in my local grocery store looking for limes. There I saw a young Hispanic woman pushing her six-month-old baby who seemed dirty and scruffy. The thought came to mind as I watched her closely, desiring what she had: "You should give me your baby!" I wanted to yell. "I would take much better care of her."

The anger and anguish filled my being until finally I took a walk along the beach in North Carolina with a wise grandmother who gently spoke God's words to me, she said, "You can be a mother right now. There are many ways in which you can mother." A glimpse of light, a little bit of hope and possibility entered my heart. I finally believed that I might be able to fulfill my dream of motherhood.

At the time, Andrew's parents were foster parents caring for medically fragile babies in Morristown, New Jersey. They had two babies in their home and were great examples of being parents in a different way! After a lot of talking, Andrew and I decided to take a leap of faith down an unknown path. It seemed a lot easier for Andrew than it was for me. As I look back, there were many fears stopping me from taking the first step over my bridge of faith. There were feelings of failure that held me back, including failure as a woman that my body was not functioning as it should. I also had many questions such as: *Can I love someone else's child? What if things don't work out?* and *How will I be able to let go and move on?* It seemed so unfair that pregnancy was not happening for me. I felt that having children was something women were meant to do, designed to do—something *I* was designed to do! These feelings of failure and fear were a great stumbling block for me.

We were quickly licensed as foster parents in Arizona. It seemed like a safe route, as we could stop at any time. Oh, how little I knew about myself!

Benjamin

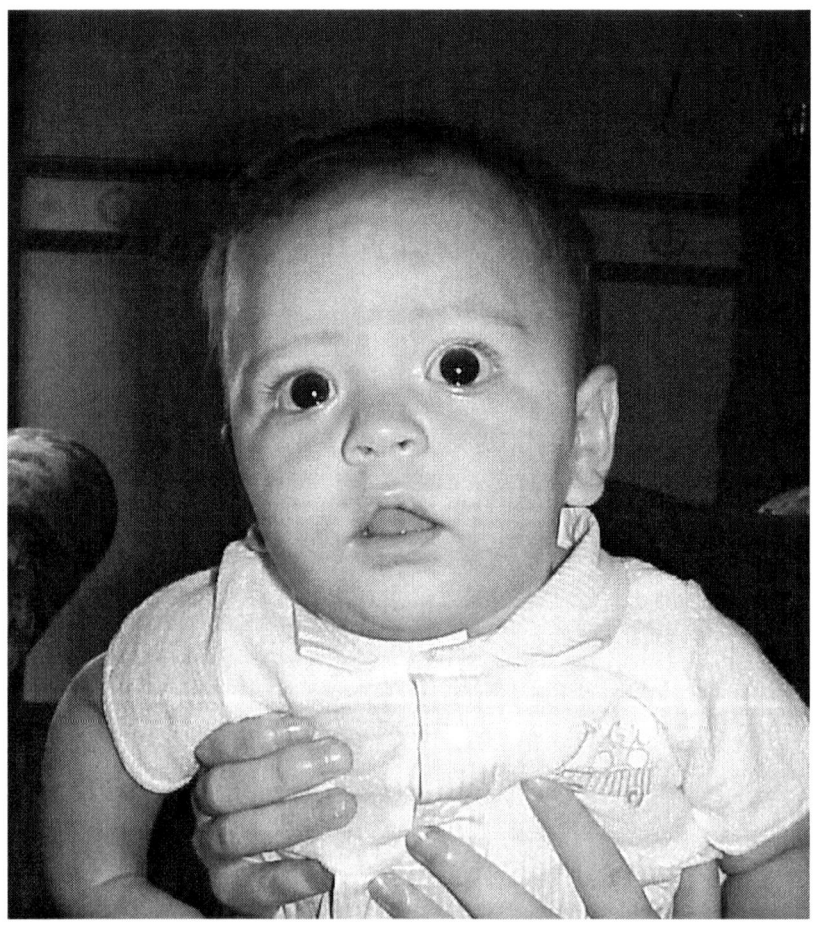

On August 15 we got a call about a six-month-old baby boy whose name was Benjamin. What joy and excitement filled my soul. We quickly went to the shelter to pick him up. The minute I saw this chubby, big brown-eyed, sad-faced, neglected, beautiful boy I wanted to keep him forever. He truly melted my heart; all those fears, concerns, and doubts just dissipated like vapor into thin air. I was truly the happiest person alive. I finally had a baby to love. I was a mother at last!

Benjamin

A sweet spirit enters our home
Just a few months here from his heavenly home.
His deep ocean eyes
And sallow skin,
Give us joy deep within.

His cute little smile
And the light in his eyes,
Radiate for a mile.
His piercing looks
And his gentle touch,
Let's us know he loves us much.

His beautiful soft skin
And his hair so thin
We wonder where he has been.
With gentle hugs
And butterfly kisses,
Our son is eternally with us.

Deana Coreen Kastello (9/08/1999)

All of my fears about this little boy truly came to pass. As I look back I can see how God was preparing me. He knew this little boy whom we adored and loved was not going to be with us long. During that time I would play a special song called "Mary's Lullaby." The song is about Mary cradling and rocking her son, the Savior, just as I was cradling and rocking Benjamin. In the chorus Mary sings, "For you are a King, but tonight you are mine." Every time I heard those words tears would just stream down my face. My spirit knew that my time with Benjamin was precious. Never have I prayed for or longed for something to work out as much as I did with Benjamin. Many prayers and tears were shed regarding him.

It had been a rocky road from the beginning to the end! Just picking him up that first day seemed disorganized. Caseworker after caseworker, visits with his mom who would just waltz in and out of his life, and finally two grandparents whom he had never known stepped into his life.

At twenty-two months he was no longer that sad-faced, stern looking boy who would just lay quietly in his crib. Instead he was a happy, normal child, getting into everything and doing what two-year-olds do. He was just an angel.

December 13 is a day I will never forget. As we drove heartbroken to a lonely parking lot in Phoenix, Benjamin was happily sleeping, oblivious to what was about to happen. We pulled up to the car that Benjamin was about to enter. There we reluctantly unstrapped him and gently handed him over to the grandparents he hardly knew. Letting go was one of the hardest things I have ever done. I had a little glimpse that night into what it must feel like when a birth mother places her baby into the unknown arms of another. With a hole in my heart we said, "Good-bye." We felt like we had just experienced a death.

If only that night I could have known the future! Little did I know that our good-bye was only for a moment, a short time. Roughly two years later we had just returned to the United States after spending time in medical school in Grenada, West Indies. We received a very unexpected phone call from the attorney who had fought so hard for us to keep Benjamin. She was calling to tell us that a friend of hers from law school had contacted her about adopting a little boy called Benjamin—immediately our attorney knew she had to contact us. In my heart I instantly felt like jumping on a plane and going to get him! We were so excited just to find out that he was safe and well. We learned that Benjamin had been placed with a wonderful family who loved him. Even though Andrew and I did not want to let go of him a second time, we both knew that Benjamin was where he was meant to be. His new family was the only family he remembered and now loved. The void in our hearts from that lonely night in that Phoenix parking lot was suddenly filled with gratitude and love with the knowledge that our little boy Benjamin was happy and loved by not only us but his new family.

We have had the wonderful opportunity of meeting Benjamin's family a number of times. The tears of love that both his mother and I have shed on these occasions have truly bonded us together. Seeing Benjamin again and being able to talk with him whenever we want is and has been the greatest gift we could have ever received. It has not only been very healing for us but for Benjamin as well.

Our father in heaven does know and love his children.

It is hard to trust in the Lord's ways instead of our own. But he truly knows what he is doing with each of us.

> For my thoughts are not your thoughts,
> Neither are your ways my ways, saith the Lord.
> Isaiah 55:8

Ben's Story

I am writing this story for Ben and for his first "Real Mom," (Deana)—the Mom who saved him from the loneliness of being deprived of family love when he was only a baby of around six months old. And of course, I am also writing for all Real Moms who long to realize the love God intended for us to share with our children.

Benjamin came into our lives when he was just a little older than three years. I had been praying for a sister or brother for Christopher, who was four, and whom we had adopted when he was just a year old. I had contacted my Christian Family Care caseworker and informed her that we were ready for a new foster placement. Two days later, I was at work when I got the call. A little boy needed a home as soon as possible. My husband, LeRoy, was on a backpacking/hiking/fishing trip on the Black River. There was no way to reach him, or to get his permission for us to add a new member to our family. But, fortunately, I knew my husband well. I knew the breadth and the power of his love, and that he would permit me to make such an important decision for our family in a time of need.

My heart raced. It was a little after the lunch hour, and I agreed that I would meet the caseworker at Benjamin's day care at about 3:30 PM. I left work early to pick up Chris at his day care and drove as quickly as I could carefully drive directly to Ben's day care. I got there before the caseworker, and took Chris inside. We tried to wait patiently. On the way over, I had asked Chris if he would like a brother. He had been an only child for a year, since his two foster brothers had been placed in an adoption home. He had loved having all of our attention, but he was also lonely for his brothers, who had been with us for two years. We were all very lonely for the two boys, whom we still loved so much. I knew Chris was ready to share his life with a new brother.

When we met Ben, he was eager to come home with us. He had been in a foster home with nine children, and it had not been a good placement for him. The parents had too many children to give Ben the love and attention needed by a child of his age. Ben adjusted to our home very quickly, and seemed to be thriving and secure. The two boys were becoming close playmates, and I could not wait for my husband to come home. He could not be reached by telephone, so he was in for a big surprise. When he arrived home three days later, he was tired and dirty from a week of camping. Ben greeted him at the front door with "Hi, Dad!" I was in the kitchen and heard the greeting. When I came out to greet him, LeRoy's face was incredulous. I said, "Hey, Dad, this is our son Ben." He raised his eyebrows and his tired eyes twinkled as he greeted Ben. We were a family at last.

I have always taught our boys that Real Parents are the ones who give them Real Love (see the book *Real Love in Parenting* by Greg Baehr). As time went on, I learned more about Ben's life. I was blessed with the opportunity to meet his biological grandmother, who was actually younger than me. She told me about his birth parents, siblings, and his first Real Mom, Deana, who had loved him well and taught him to be helpful, respectful, and self-respecting. These qualities defined Ben from the beginning and helped him to become an independent and compassionate child at a very early age. Ben is now nine years old, in the third grade. He is witty and smart, and has a deep sense of fairness and a dedication to making the world a better place for the weak in spirit. He champions the underdog and really cares about fighting for justice. He wants to be a professional soccer player and a soldier, to fight for his country and then to be a public defender. Ben wrote the following poem when he was in the second grade, for Valentine's Day:

Love

Love is beautiful things and someone giving you flowers
And sweet kids wandering around.
Love is the taste of chocolate;
Hershey bars and ice cream smell like love.
When my parents hug me it makes me feel loved,
Love is the sound of someone laughing and my brother saying hi to me.
Love is many things, as in kids having fun,
And someone getting married.
My animals are love.
My family is also love.
Love is the whole world.

Ben Johnson

February 2007

A year ago my dad died and Ben asked me recently if I miss him, and if it makes me sad. I said that I do, and it does, but that he is always with me, and that he is my guardian angel, and guides my decisions. Ben asked me how you can know who your guardian angel is, and if it can be someone who hasn't died. I said that if you listen closely, sometimes you can recognize who is guiding and protecting you, and that I think that it can be someone who is still living. Ben thought for a moment, and said that he has two guardian angels—he believes that one is Coreen, his first Real Mom, and he doesn't know who the other one is yet.

From the beginning, I understood that my children were miracles of life. From the moment of their appearance in my life, I accepted their destiny as separate from my own and have stood in awe of them. The very fact that they survived the awesome struggle of birth and had the strength to grasp the first breath of life was the fulfillment of my greatest desire for them. Everything since has been simply an experience of joy for me. I've never assumed any honor or glory for their inner beauty or accomplishments. I praise God for the joy of letting me be such an important part of their lives. At first, I did not feel worthy of exercising my influence on their beliefs, although many times I tried. I knew from the start that I was blessed with a divine gift so grand as to change my course and fulfill my own destiny in their shadows. With time I have come to feel worthy of the role God has given me as their Real Mother. I thank God for each moment of their lives shared with me.

Pam Johnson

Daniel: He Is Patient and Honorable

Families

Families are here on earth
As we can clearly see
I like spending time with my own family
Lots of people know we live from birth to old
Born as babies
Sometimes adopted
As I was told

I like my family
Like birds love to sing
Like lions love to roar and roam
Like frogs love to hop
And toads love to breathe
Families are stuck together
Like an endless string.

Daniel Kastello (age 8)

After a lot of turmoil in the foster-care system, I quickly realized that I needed a baby to keep. The stress of Benjamin's situation and my fear of losing him were overwhelming.

We agreed to do whatever it took to get our child. On a Sunday in November of 1999 we finally talked to our bishop and asked for the Church papers to start the adoption process; something I had not been ready for until Benjamin!

Just four days later, the windows of heaven smiled down upon us. We received a call from our state foster care social worker asking if we would be interested in a baby boy. Even though he would be coming through the foster care system something inside me just yelled, "*Yes*!" Within a couple of hours, Daniel's state caseworker showed up at our door, sat us down and quite frankly said, "I'm really looking for a foster/adoption home for this child." Tears filled my eyes; I couldn't believe my ears. I just knew deep in my heart and soul that this was our son. Our loving Father in heaven was sending him to us after hearing our many heart-felt prayers. I had instant love for this little baby whom I didn't even know. Daniel's caseworker warned us of possible health problems with him but it didn't seem to matter.

By 7 PM that Thursday night our little baby arrived. He was as tiny and scrawny as could be. With a mop of jet black hair and the sweetest little face ever. I just wanted to hold him. He was wearing a white baby gown. His only belongings were a diaper bag, a bottle, a change of clothes and formula. Finally my little bundle of joy was here.

Daniel is now is now eight years old. He is the joy of my life. He's kind, sensitive, smart, responsible and obedient. He has integrity like I have never seen before. I am the blessed one as he teaches me so much. How grateful I am that God entrusted this beautiful child to me.

Elahanna: God Is Gracious

Elahanna

Beautiful petite Elahanna
Your smile so sweet.
Your twinkling blue eyes and your little feet.
Your long dark flowing hair,
And the tender love we share!
I want you to know how much I care.

As you sit and wait for your time on earth
With heavenly friends and many playmates.
The eternal love that doth abound
The peace, the kindness and so much more.
The lamb and the lion, which will lie together
Feeling the eternal love that binds us forever.

A heavenly place is where you abide
I only wish I could be at your side.
To see your gaze, to feel your touch
And tell you how I miss you much.
I miss the knowledge I once knew

Yet I know my work is here for you!

*I sense your impatience
And desire to come.
I see you sitting, wondering and waiting.
Dressed in white, with an aura so bright
A beautiful angelic face and your warm embrace.*

Deana Kastello (1997)

Elahanna was truly a gift from God. On the previous page is a poem I wrote in 1997. I had been meditating one bright sunny day while alone in our little house in Arizona. As I just sat, pondered, and meditated over the things I had been praying about, all of a sudden in my mind's eye, I saw a five-year-old girl standing before me, dressed in white. It was as clear and real as the day. She had long dark hair and was sweet and kind. Her spirit was so strong and I just felt her longing to come to me. I knew that this was my future child.

I also assumed at that time that she would be my birth child. During the following four years I thought about her constantly and continued to feel her yearning for me as much as I yearned for her. The bond I felt with her was so real and powerful. That day on my couch was when the conception in my heart began, with nothing but love and desire for her.

Little did I know, the reason for the vision was because Elahanna was not going to enter life through my womb, but through the womb of somebody else.

On January 24, 2001, the unexpected happened. My sweet husband had just left for medical school in Grenada ten days earlier. I was unable to leave as Daniel had not been officially adopted yet. I was in the midst of selling our home and moving into an apartment. With all this change in our lives were unprepared for what was about to happen. I received a call around 7 PM from my neighbor's sister who informed me that she was pregnant. She wanted to know if we wanted her baby. I had to sit down. My whole body shook with shock; I couldn't believe my ears. I knew instantly that this was my Elahanna, even though the sex of the baby had not been confirmed yet. I quickly called Andrew; we truly felt blessed.

Miracles happen today and this was one of my many miracles. I can hardly describe my feelings toward this sweet, selfless girl who had just presented us with the greatest gift we could have ever wanted. We couldn't believe this was happening to us. With the four month warning of another child joining our growing family I had the wonderful opportunity of attending doctor's appointments, seeing ultra sounds and, best of all, getting to know this birth mother. I had the privilege of being not only her friend but also her coach during the long painful hours of labor. What a gift!

During this time I had learned that breast-feeding was possible as an adoptive parent. Having never been pregnant, the doctor I saw said it would be a great undertaking and that it might not work. With the desire to experience as much of motherhood as I could, I took hormones and many herbs and I pumped like a cow for six weeks before the birth. Hardly a drop of milk came from my breast; I was feeling quite discouraged.

Finally the day arrived, May 29, 2001, when the pangs of labor took over this sweet birth mother. Andrew had just returned from school for the birth and the summer. We watched helplessly as this young girl battled through her pain to allow this little life to enter the world. It was humbling and heartbreaking to watch her suffer and do all the physical hard work, only to hold her baby for a short time.

As Andrew severed the cord that bound them both to each other, this mother, devastated and heartbroken, just cradled her baby for the last time knowing how every minute was precious. Finally the dreaded moment she had been preparing for came. Through many tears she gently and lovingly placed this precious gift into my arms. It was a bittersweet moment for us both. A moment we will never forget.

As I received our baby into my arms I was overwhelmed by the love I felt for this courageous birth mom, who could have easily had an abortion, but instead she took the hard yet higher road in life. She loved her child and wanted the best for her. There was such power in this act of selflessness and sacrifice as she handed Elahanna to me. She is the mother who gave Elahanna the gift of life, and I am the mother who has the blessing of loving her, teaching, and nurturing her all of her life.

Yes I was able to breast-feed my baby. I had a small supply of breast milk and I supplemented also. I breast-fed for nine months. It was a great accomplishment. It was definitely a lot of work, but worth every bit of it.

It was a great bonding experience for us both.

Elahanna and Daniel were both adopted on the same day just six weeks after Elahanna's birth. Elahanna is now six years old and just a joy. She is smart, witty, and fun, with a lot of spunk. She is a thinker, deep and sensitive. She is kind and likes to please and help with her siblings. Most of all, she is especially close to me, her mother.

Noah Michael: What An Angel!

I prayed for this child, and the Lord has granted me what I asked of him.
1 Samuel 1:27

Noah's story began when we arrived in Grenada as a family of four. One Sunday afternoon after church, Daniel, who was twenty months old at the time and could barely talk, was napping. It was quiet in our home when all of a sudden we heard Daniel talking and calling "Michael, Michael!" Our ears perked up as we looked at each other in wonderment, questioning who he was calling for. It was definitely a Michael and it was as if the boy was in the room with him.

We thought no more about this unusual experience until returning to the United States. Daniel was now three years old. One week early in the winter months, every night at the same time Daniel would start to cry and inform me that a boy kept coming into his room. At first I wasn't sure what to think and wondered if there was a restless ghost in our home. After ruling out all other possibilities I honestly felt that this experience was very real. I knew in my heart that a boy was coming next, maybe it was baby Michael.

After much praying and talking, Andrew and I decided to get licensed in New Jersey as foster parents. We also made the decision to go through our church adoption agency, even though they had informed us that our chances were very slim of getting a baby through them at that time. Two weeks after we received our foster care license we got a call about an abandoned, drug-addicted baby boy who was three weeks old and needed a home.

I had a feeling of peace come over me in spite of all the drugs this little boy had been exposed to. I knew without any doubt that this baby was our son. We told Daniel in the kitchen that we were going to get a baby—he jumped up and down with joy, shouting "It's baby Michael! It's baby Michael!"

That very day we went to see him. There were about thirty babies in the border baby room; we had no idea what he looked like. However, off in the corner I spotted a tiny little guy who was just gorgeous. The next thing I knew they were placing this beautiful angel in my arms.

The joy and happiness I felt as I held my little Noah is indescribable. Any fear of long-term drug effects were not even a thought; I truly felt as I held him that he was a special gift from God.

Noah did have drug withdrawals for quite some time. We did a lot of baby massage with him, which helped greatly. He was our only baby that we could not hold for too long because it over-stimulating him, causing tremors and anxiousness. By the time he was six months old, all withdrawals had finally stopped.

Noah came to us with no name, but we knew instantly that this was our baby Michael that Daniel had been preparing us for. Noah has brought so much laughter, lightheartedness, and sweetness into our family. He has the best sense of humor and is just a bundle of laughs. For someone who entered the world with trauma and addiction, he is just happy to be alive—a true breath of fresh air.

Noah is now four years old and is just beautiful inside and out. He can be active at times yet he is sweet, tender, and kind hearted. He is extremely smart and is already reading. He likes to be challenged and shocks us daily with his abilities. Noah is a miracle and he is a true testimony of what love can do. Noah is our beacon of light. We love and adore him to pieces.

Halle Joan: Our Sweet, Tender Little Heart.

My Heaven

Heaven, what is heaven? One might ask
Heaven's on earth with a glorious task!
Just look around and you will see
In simple pleasures, there are many hidden treasures
Heaven is the twinkle in your child's eye
Joy, innocence, beauty, love unfeigned
These are the things we cannot buy.
Within these heaven-sent eyes
There's a love that eternally binds
My heart skips a beat as I fall to my knees
What have I done to be worthy?
Of such incomprehensible love indeed.

It is heaven when they cry for you
And no one else, only you can ease their pain
And help it all make sense
Heaven is when tiny arms wrap themselves around your neck
That almost makes you fall to the deck.
Wiggles, giggles, and many scribbles
Their cheeky smiles would have you take a trip
Instead you only have wine to sip!
As it takes everything you have to bite your lip
Love notes often find their way on torn pieces of paper
With love words and funny faces
Beautiful red hearts scattered all over
These notes warm my heart and give me a fresh New Start
So I can continue to do my part
There lie my treasures greatest of all
As tiny handprints, markers, and all
Imprint my walls.

My children are my life all in all
Without them I would be in strife
As I would not be able to fulfill my life
Heaven heard my many heartfelt prayers
And decided to send me a herd!
What joy they are all five
They keep me bouncing, full of life
I thank heaven and all its help
But most of all my Heavenly Father, himself
The windows of heaven truly opened
And down showered blessings too many to be spoken.

Deana Coreen Kastello

❋ ❋ ❋

Four months after Noah came home I had a dream. I dreamed of a little girl standing beside me. I didn't see her face, but she had a very strong presence in the dream. I knew once again that this was a daughter of mine. Her name was also revealed to me in this dream.

After this experience I couldn't stop feeling that my daughter was coming! Once again conception in my heart had begun. My love for her was immediate and all-consuming, though I had no idea how or when would she get here. I would mentally slap myself and say "you have a baby, relax." The growing was already taking place.

In September, just four months after my dream, an unexpected email came. It was from a young girl in Arizona who was pregnant. She had found our profile through our church adoption agency on the Internet, which had been posted by accident. We had already informed them in January of the arrival of Noah.

When my sweet husband read the email he was overcome with emotion. He knew in his heart that this was our daughter. We quickly responded to the email by telling this birth mother that we had already added to our family, but were very interested. After several bumps here and there, she insisted that we were the family for her unborn child.

Once again the window of heaven was showering down blessings. It was completely unexpected. My husband was in his fourth year of medical school; we had no money. Stress was high due to exams, and we still did not know where we would be doing a residency in the next few months. People thought we were crazy! We felt a sense of disapproval from those around us, but we couldn't deny what we felt and knew in our hearts to be right. Both of us had it confirmed that this child was our daughter. We knew that God had a plan and would not give us more than we could handle.

The day after Thanksgiving our beautiful sweet daughter Halle was born.

Another brave, selfless birth mom made the hard choice—for the love of her child—giving her the gift of life. Once more, with a heavy heart, I reached out my arms and she reached out hers and placed this innocent little person, our daughter, into my arms I was so humbled. What great trust she had in us that we would love and care for this child. What faith these women have who hand their babies to other mothers. This birth mom was so in tune with the plan of God for her and for Halle.

Halle is now three years old and is the sweetest, kindest person in our family. Her eyes radiate kindness, gentleness, and love. She is deep, with lots of emotion. She enjoys her dolls and is extremely nurturing. She is nothing but love and joy. Halle has been such a gift to us.

God surely works in mysterious ways! In Isaiah 55:8 it reads, "For my thoughts are not your thoughts, neither are your ways my ways, saith the lord." It takes great faith to trust in God's ways and not our own. He has a much greater plan for us than we have for ourselves. You can rise to the occasion; you can fulfill your life's purpose and have the desires of your heart. You can handle much more than you think you can. You can live in joy and happiness, basking in the inner fulfillment you seek.

May God bless you as you step onto your bridge of faith.

Looking back I can see a clear distinction: it was not "being a mother" as much as the experience of pregnancy that I desired. We can be mothers in many different ways. It could be a donation to a third world country, or by mothering nieces, nephews, friends, and neighbors.

It was as clear as night and day that it was having the experience of doing what women are uniquely designed to do—give birth—that I had been seeking.

While waiting in Arizona for our clearance to leave with our four-day-old Halle, I had a light bulb moment! I realized that I had been experiencing pregnancy with each of my four children. It just didn't happen in my *womb* it happened in my *heart*. This realization was an answer to my prayers. I finally got it!

Saraya: A Miracle!

Is anything too hard for the Lord?
Genesis 17:14

Just two months later—Valentine's Day to be exact—I had felt the normal pre-menstrual cramps and was just waiting for my period to start. That morning I couldn't help but think, *Oh, how romantic it would be if I were pregnant on Valentine's Day.* Of course I knew I wasn't, but it was Valentine's Day! There was still that little bit of hope and wishful thinking of wanting to become pregnant.

I went over it again and again. *When did my period actually start?* I had given up on keeping track. After thinking about it all morning, I decided to take one more pregnancy test. I had taken so many tests over the nine years of my infertility that I decided *Aw, what the heck! What's one more test? Just a few dollars lost.*

So with that thought in mind I quickly ran to the drug store just to put my mind at ease once more. I came home and took the test with complete peace of mind. All of a sudden my eyes lit up and my heart skipped a few beats. Was I reading this test correctly? There was no longer one line, but *two*! I couldn't believe my eyes. *How can this be possible?* I kept repeating in my mind.

I quickly called my mother, panicking in shock and disbelief. It took five tests to convince me I was really pregnant.

Our Valentine's Day in 2005 will never be forgotten. Andrew and I both acted like zombies! We were so taken aback. Here we were with a five-year-old, a three-year-old, a one-year-old and a two-and-a-half-month-old. We were moving to who-knew-where for a surgery residency. And now we were pregnant. After all those tears and overwhelming feelings of wanting to conceive, my reaction was certainly not what I thought it was going to be. I have to admit we both felt very overwhelmed and afraid of how we were going to manage. After surviving the first few months of nausea—and in the meantime moving to a new state with four children under the age of six!—I finally had the chance to enjoy this miracle I had been waiting for for so many years.

It was a wonderful experience. What amazed me the most was how a life is created from a tiny little sperm that makes it to an egg! How it literally starts out as nothing. This to me was the most amazing part—to really understand the miracle of life itself. But at the same time, I realized that it's the growth of the baby that is important, not where it was born.

Saraya is now a spunky two-and-a-half-year-old. She is beautiful, affectionate, and very sensitive. She is smart and very funny. The whole family adores her, and her siblings, especially, cannot get enough of her and continue to spoil her. Saraya was another wonderful unexpected gift.

Conceiving in the Heart

Conceiving in the heart is very similar to pregnancy—it all starts with a tiny seed. Maybe a little bit of hope and possibility, thoughts that develop into research on different options. The seed is grown by steps being taken: a phone call, asking for paperwork and finger prints, getting background checks and references, taking classes in some cases, and seminars. All these steps enlarge the seed that has been planted in your heart. As each month passes the excitement and joy kick in. You are so much closer to your dream of parenthood.

Just like a nine-month pregnancy, where a fully grown life exists in your womb, there is also a fully grown life force that develops deep and real, in your heart. Just like a pregnancy there can be challenges, complications, bed rest, tiredness, and pain at the end. Adoption is no walk in the park either! There are many bumps in the road that cause pain and suffering, confusion at times, frustration, tiredness, red tape, long plane rides, mix-ups, money, and time.

It all takes work; there is no easy road when it comes to having the family you desire. We have to do our part, just like the long hours of labor can take their toll, so can the emotional roller coaster of adoption be just as intense. "I didn't say it would be easy. I just said it would be worth it"

For all of you out there who are in the depths of despair: doing *nothing* is the worst thing you can do. Think about the following question: do you want a baby or a pregnancy? There is a big difference. I am going to guess that some of you who are reading this and answering this question, if you are truly honest, probably desire a pregnancy. To be able to experience life inside your womb, feel the movement inside your growing belly, morning sickness, and even labor, *yes* even that.

Stop right here, let go, all of the above is wonderful, but it is not what matters most. This is such a small part of becoming a parent. Keep your focus on the bigger picture, your child. Focusing on nine months of pregnancy stops you from seeing the bigger picture and stops you from taking the necessary steps forward so you can have the joy and happy times, such as holding and playing with your children, cuddling with them, doing homework with them, seeing them in plays, and watching them grow into amazing people! Most of all, enjoying the unconditional love that only children really know how to give. Only children can teach us about patience, about ourselves. They show us our weaknesses so they can become strengths.

Please let go and let the seed in your heart begin to grow, that's all it takes.

Deana Coreen Kastello

The Life of Gabrielle

For all that I am
I owe to my mother.

I look back on my childhood and thank the stars above.
For everything you gave me, but mostly for your love.
—Wayne F. Winters

To this day I still consider myself blessed that I grew up in a foster family.

Whenever I look back to when I was little, I find it extremely difficult to pinpoint any happy memories. My past was never filled with loving hugs and kisses. In fact, until the age of five I had never heard the words "I love you" in any way directed toward me.

Most people would agree that the first five years of your life are the most critical in your development. Unfortunately, these happened to be the worst five years of my life. During these years my parents were at the prime of their drug and alcohol addictions.

My father would come home drunk practically every night. As I lie in my bed, I would be forced to witness my mother being beaten and abused. I would lie awake most nights with my brother and sister and cry as we listened to and watched her scream while the combination of blood and tears ran down her face.

What hurt the most was not what he did, but the fact that there was nothing that we could do to prevent it from happening. My mother was too scared of my father and what could mere children do against a monster such as that?

When I got older my mother and I seemed to get closer. She quickly became my best friend. She would tell me all the time that one day she would take me away from our nightmare and we could finally be a real family. The closer I got to my mom, the more I would be abused.

When my dad would come home drunk in the afternoon and my other siblings were at school, I tried to help my mom. I knew that a five-year-old couldn't protect her, but I could distract my dad to draw the attention away from her. It worked almost all the time.

Most nights he would get too exhausted to abuse her after giving me simple cuts and bruises. I didn't care what happened to me; as long as my mother was okay, it didn't matter.

When I had just turned five, my mom finally had the strength and courage to leave my dad. She went to a shelter and hid from him. My dad was charged with domestic violence and told that if he ever did anything rash toward us or took us out of the state where they couldn't watch him, the state would take us away. My dad didn't want to cooperate with the state and definitely not the government. In late August 1995, he kidnapped my three siblings and me and took us to our grandma's house in Missouri.

We stayed there around two and a half weeks before the state found us and took us away. I remember that day clearly. They came into my classroom and took me away at school. I cried so much and I started screaming. I did not want to leave again. I liked it in Missouri. It was far away from the life I had before. After I got into the car, they picked up my brothers and sister. We stopped at my grandma's house for about five minutes. I couldn't even grab my clothes or belongings. I only had enough time to grab one stuffed animal and a small blanket. I was so scared. I didn't understand what was happening to me. I didn't feel safe. I was in a car with complete strangers for hours. It was almost complete silence the whole way back to Iowa.

That night, my siblings and I were split up for the first time. My older sister and I went to one foster home, my brother Sean to another, and my oldest brother Bobby was placed in a group home. (Many foster parents aren't willing to take in teenagers. He was sixteen and it is very hard to place children that old.)

I remember getting to my foster home very late. We were greeted warmly and welcomed with open arms. It was way too much to take in at once. I was scared, tired, and angry. I wanted to wake up and have it all be a dream. If only life were so easy, huh? I knew I wasn't alone with my feelings of uneasiness. As I lay awake in my bed I could hear soft sobs and restless tossing and turning from my sister just a couple feet below me.

As the months and years progressed we began to fit in with the family and I would talk to my mom on the phone. Life, it seemed, was getting better at last.

My mom moved out of the shelter and got her own apartment. My brother turned eighteen and moved out into the apartment with my mom. After living in a few foster homes, Sean came to live with my sister and me at our foster home. This meant everything to us because family had always been the most important thing in life. We were almost all together again.

We would have visits with my mom weekly and I would get hugged and kissed. My mom would frequently tell me that she loved me. Being loved is the best feeling in the world when you have been abused or neglected for so long. I started to believe that maybe it would be a happy ending after all.

Our family took a devastating turn when I was seven. My mother, whom I had loved most in the entire world, died. After this happened I was severely depressed. I was so scared that I would forget her hugs and kisses, how she looked, and how much we had loved each other.

I was angry with the world and God. The anger, with time, turned to sadness and then finally, to acceptance. I knew that I would always love her and I realized that not even death can obscure the love we once had.

Before she died, my birth mother made good friends with my foster mom. I know now that this is rare in the foster care system. When my foster mom talks about her, she talks as if they were the best of friends. My foster mom promised to take good care of us and love us as if we were her own kids, so when my mom died, my foster mom knew that she would adopt us, as a last promise to my mom.

My dad's rights were terminated when I was nine and shortly afterwards I was adopted along with my brother Sean. My sister chose not to be adopted because she was sixteen and more scholarships and college aid are available for teens who age out.

I have been with my adoptive family twelve years now and I would not have chosen any other family to have in my life. Their love and care has meant so much to me, and although I will never have my birth mom again, every time I hug my adoptive mom it takes me back to her. It reminds me of how my family has never given up on me. It reminds me of our love. It makes me realized that her promise was never broken. I finally have a real family.

Gabrielle

Gabby is currently a senior in high school and plans to attend college upon graduation. She wants to teach English and participate in music performance. Gabby and her siblings remain in close contact with each other and she also is able to maintain a connection with her extended biological family. Gabby advocates for change within the foster care system by speaking for a group called Elevate, a program of Children & Families of Iowa. This program is a group of young people who seek to inspire others to new levels of understanding and compassion to the life connection needs of foster care and adoptive teens by sharing their personal stories of hope. Through this program Gabby is able to speak with public officials and the community about her experience and ways to improve the system for the future.

Dear Birth Parent

The Apple of Our Eyes

How do we love you?
Let us count the ways
We love your spirit
So lively, so adventurous, and so loving
We love your golden hair
And your laugh that turns your eyes into crescent moons
We love being your mommy and daddy
Seeing how you grow and learn
Most of all we love you because you are you
You are the apple of our eyes
Our very special Lily.

Eleanor

In the summer of 1999 my husband Matt and I were undergoing what we had decided would be our last series of fertility treatments. It had been six years since we had begun trying to start a family. I was now thirty-two years old and Matt was thirty-six. Initially we were patient, understanding that my endometriosis could make becoming pregnant difficult, but not impossible. As time went by, however, our frustrations grew. The invasive tests, treatments, and surgeries were draining us emotionally and physically, and we were no closer to our dream of becoming parents.

In August when the third round of fertility treatments proved unsuccessful we decided it was time to open the door to adoption. Over the years we had become comfortable with adoption. We both felt that biological ties were not essential for loving a child. We were also fortunate to learn about adoption from a close friend who was an adoption social worker. She educated us upon the different types of adoption and the legal issues involved, and helped dispel some of the myths associated with adoption. By September we had selected an adoption agency and were beginning to complete our home study, the process of becoming approved to adopt. We had chosen to pursue a domestic adoption.

August and September were a time of transition for Matt and me. As the adoption community was welcoming us in, we found ourselves dealing with the fact that we could not conceive. I struggled to close that door, it meant missing what I had always looked forward to—seeing in our children the image of Matt and glimpsing the personality of the little boy that his mom had so endearingly described. Even during those times, a strong feeling would always counterbalance my sense of loss—the feeling of hope that perhaps our baby had already been conceived.

During the fall we completed our home study. We then began to write a "Dear Birth Parent" letter, which consisted of descriptions of ourselves, our lifestyles, and our interests. This profile, including photographs, was then added to our agency's adoption book for birth parents to read. We also met with several adoption attorneys who also accepted our profile. Then we waited.

One Monday afternoon the following May we received news that a birth mother had chosen us to adopt her baby. Wow! We could not believe this was happening so soon, we had expected the wait would be longer. To our amazement we also learned that the birth mother was overdue by a week and that she could deliver the baby at any time.

The agency shared with us all the information they had. The fifteen-year old birth mother, Anna, and her mother Rose had met with an adoption attorney that day and they had seen our profile. Anna lived with her mother just twenty miles away. Anna had hidden her pregnancy until her third trimester, and therefore had only recently begun to receive prenatal care. According to her doctors both baby and mother were healthy. As for the birth father, he had apparently broken up with Anna when he learned of her pregnancy. Anna expressed that she did not want to meet with us, but would like us to be at the hospital during the delivery so that the baby could come straight to us.

The agency wanted to meet with us the next day. They suggested we start thinking of baby names! Something so wonderful was happening, we were elated, ecstatic.

One of the most remarkable feelings we experienced that day was the honor we felt that Anna had chosen us to adopt her baby. From all the couples in the profile books, she chose us. It is the most uplifting feeling to know that a perfect stranger could touch your life so profoundly.

On Thursday morning Anna was in labor, and we were on our way to the hospital. As we walked through the hospital we felt very nervous, not knowing what to expect or how we would be received by the nursing staff or the birth family. Arriving on the maternity floor it relieved us to know that the nursing staff was expecting us. They quickly informed us about Anna, telling us that everything was going well, but slowly. The staff had prepared a room so the baby could come straight to us.

One thing about learning that you're about to become parents in a matter of days—there's very little time to prepare. The only thing we had for a baby was a crib in the attic! On that Thursday morning as I waited at the hospital, Matt took a list that we had made to Babies 'R Us. We needed everything: bottles, formula, clothes, car seat, bassinet, diapers, and so forth. So much for my dream of coordinating everything for the baby; now it was simply a matter of getting everything, and quick!

Over the course of the day Matt and I met with Anna's parents. Their warmth and openness put us at ease. Their deep concern for Anna was apparent as we talked. We all felt the weight of the situation and the implications for Anna, both immediate and long-term. Her parents talked about Anna as an excellent student, very lively, social, and beautiful, as we had seen in the photos of her. We learned too that it was Anna's decision to choose adoption. She wanted to complete high school and go to college. We were thrilled to learn these details about Anna, something we could share with the baby at a later date.

After a long and difficult labor, Rose knocked on our door. The baby was here and *she* was in the nursery. It was a little girl!

What a selfless gesture from Rose to be the person to tell us the news and to lead us, running with us up the hallway, to the baby. She was truly happy for us, managing somehow to reserve the sorrow that would surely come and share in the joy of this new life. In that moment it was all about the baby—Matt, Rose, Anna's grandmother, and I all looking through the small window of the nursery door, her little pink face peeping over the blanket that swaddled her—she was beautiful. And when Anna's grandmother asked if we had chosen a name for her, I said "Lily Catherine," and mentioned that Lily had been my grandmother's name. What brought fresh tears to our eyes and joy to our hearts was Rose's response that Catherine had been her grandmother's name. And so Lily Catherine received a truly fitting name.

Shortly, a nurse came to evaluate Lily. She invited us all to accompany her, and it was at this point that Rose magnanimously stepped back. She wanted this to be our experience only.

There she was, our daughter, lying in a little crib. We could see ten tiny perfect fingers and ten tiny perfect toes. She was so peaceful and calm. We watched bewildered and amazed as the nurse completed her evaluation. Then finally, Lily was in my arms. The feeling of love, gratitude, wonder, and joy was almost inexplicable. And to see her in Matt's arms—my partner through this entire journey, with this child of our hopes and dreams. It was everything.

Although her initial decision was to not meet Lily, with the encouragement of the maternity social worker, suggesting that "you have to first say hello to say good-bye," Anna came to the nursery that afternoon with Rose. We understood her reluctance to meet, but were very glad she came.

When Anna walked in we were struck by her beauty and her composure. She was very attractive with long strawberry blond hair and hazel eyes. She was a little shy, but with Rose's help we had a touching conversation. We did not talk about the adoption plan or other details. We simply talked in the moment about how Anna was feeling and how Lily was doing. She smiled and looked affectionately at Lily as we talked about her. The opportunity for us to express our gratitude did not arise, nor do I think Anna wanted it to. We had written our thoughts in a letter to Anna which we gave to her as she left. The letter, or anything we could do or say, could never fully express how we admired Anna's courageous and thoughtful decision.

During our stay at the hospital we had tried to subdue our excitement out of respect for Anna and her family. The only visitors we permitted were two of our very close friends, and my sister and her husband who were visiting from Ireland. It was not until we brought Lily home that we felt fully able to celebrate. We made so many phone calls, surprising people, most of whom had no idea we had even found a birth mother. Their responses were overwhelmingly positive—everyone was thrilled to see us finally become parents.

Despite our joy, there were reservations. Anna could still change her mind and we knew we would be crushed if this happened. We were careful to remind people of this fact and asked them not to send gifts. Our friends were desperate to have a baby shower for us, but, too nervous, we asked them to wait until the birth parents went to court.

After eight weeks the court date came. Anna, true to her word, signed the papers relinquishing her parental rights. The birth father did not appear at court, and through his absence his parental rights were terminated. Lily would be our daughter forever.

We had the baby shower and celebrated with everyone. Matt's parents came from New York, and mine from England. They were delighted to have this wonderful, special baby in the family. Lily was a joy. She was such an engaging baby, full of smiles and gleeful sounds. By ten months she was walking and beginning to show a mischievous side! By two years she was starting to grow fine, blonde hair on her little bald head. And as she grew each year we noticed a pattern—whether people knew Lily was adopted or not, they commented that she looked like Matt!

In no time Lily was in preschool, then kindergarten, and today she is a terrific eight-year-old—intelligent, funny, energetic, and oh so tall! She has accepted the story of her birth as being part of what makes her special. Some day Lily would like to meet Anna and we have promised our support and help when that time comes. We think of Anna often and hope that her life is a happy one and that she was able to find comfort in her decision.

Eleanor

From My Arms to Yours

On the Wings of a Prayer

I set you free on the wings of a prayer
To fly through life in His tender care,

You're free from the nest and the ties that are bound
Free from the pressures I carry around.

If I kept you I'd only be cutting your wings,
Not offering the chance a true family brings.

The decision I've made has my heart torn in two,
But I know what I'm doing is the best thing for you.

The sky is so vast, the mountains so high
Take wing and remember: I love you.

Good-bye.

Lisa Bote-Phillips, a birth mother

We were a young couple, married for only a few years when we decided it was time to start our family. Little did we know it would take more than we thought to make that happen. After trying for a year to get pregnant with no results we sought out help and soon found out that our chances to get pregnant, even with help from in vitro fertilization (IVF), were only 2 percent. It was devastating. It didn't take us long, however, to realize that the Lord had different plans for us.

We soon started the adoption process, and boy was it a process. We were surprised to find out all that it entailed. It took us about six months to complete the process.

Our first son's adoption was such a surprise to us. Everything happened so fast! We found out that we had been chosen and two days later his birth mom was unexpectedly induced early because of complications. We got to meet her for the first time after she was released from the hospital. Our son, Jonah was at the agency with a worker, but we could not meet him yet. We had such a wonderful time getting to know our beautiful birth mom. She was so sweet and kind. We felt an instant love for and connection with her—like we had known each other forever.

We left that night elated and could not wait to see her again the next day when we would get to go back and finally meet our son. Little did we know just how hard it would be. When we went back the next day, we talked more with our birth mom and then she left the room. She was only gone for a few minutes, but it seemed much longer. Then she came in with Jonah. He was so little. Our birth mom had tears in her eyes and her face was red from crying. She handed him to me and a myriad of emotions enfolded me. I knew that this baby was mine. I knew he was meant to be in our family and that the Lord had saved him just for us. I loved him instantly! I was so happy. And as much as I was thrilled that I finally had my baby after so many years of waiting for this moment, I was sad. I was filled with grief because I knew that by taking this sweet baby home with me, I was breaking someone's heart. Someone that I hadn't known very long, but that I loved. And the most amazing thing to me was that she was not thinking about her pain, but only our happiness. She wanted more than anything to know that we were happy. There were a lot of tears shed that night as we sat and talked and as she showed us all of the things that she had learned and loved about her son in the short time that she got to be with him.

Our second son, Simon, was a totally different story. We waited forever to get him. Okay, it was really only two and a half years, but it seemed like forever. The really interesting thing about his adoption is that everything really went very smoothly. It was all of the stuff in between that was hard. You know, the waiting period. The not knowing what direction you should take. The endless comments from people about how they heard that this agency or that agency has babies that are just waiting to be adopted, only to find out that they charge way too much, or they really don't have children "just waiting." Add to that the realization that I still felt empty and didn't know why. I loved Jonah and he very much filled a place in my heart, but something still just wasn't right. I believe that one of the biggest things that people don't understand about adoption, is that it takes the pain away from wanting a child and being a parent, but it doesn't take away the feeling of loss that you feel as a woman for something that is innately yours, that of being able to get pregnant and feel that baby inside you. It has gotten easier, knowing that I will never carry a baby in my body, but I don't think that pain will ever fully go away. You can only start to heal when you recognize what is going on. My sweet Simon was the start to that recognition and healing.

We found out about him three months before he was born. Boy was that a long time to know he was coming! We got to meet with his sweet birth mom several times before he was actually born. We got to know her well and we loved when we got to see her. She made Simon a blanket and sent home many gifts for him. When Simon was placed with us, it was easier than with Jonah. Maybe because we had done it before and we knew more what to expect. Maybe because we knew his birth mom better than we had been able to get to know Jonah's. Maybe we had all had more time to prepare for this day. No matter what the reason, it was nice. We were able to focus more on Simon and talk more with his birth mom without as many tears. We were also able to meet Simon's birth dad. That was an experience that we hadn't had before and we were grateful for that opportunity. Simon was born just a few weeks before Christmas. He is the most wonderful Christmas gift that I have ever received.

Luke's adoption was different for us in many respects. We actually were not planning on adopting more. We wanted more children, but we didn't want to go through the process again. It was just too hard to think about. But Heavenly Father had different plans for us. He knew there were more children that were supposed to come to our family. He soon let us know that there was another and that we needed to be prepared. Not long after that, we were approached by someone we knew and she told us she was pregnant and wanted to know if we would adopt her baby. So the process started again, but was much smoother this time. We got to see Luke's birth mom periodically throughout her pregnancy. It was nice to spend time with her and even nicer to get to know her better. She invited us to the hospital to be there when Luke was born. That was an amazing experience. I will always be grateful to her for that. I had never seen one of my children just minutes after being born and I will never forget the experiences that I was able to have with Luke. I got to go into the nursery and watch him get his first bath. I got to feed him his very first bottle. I got to just sit and hold him in his birth mom's hospital room and talk with her about him. The most fun part of Luke's adoption is that we didn't tell our families about him. It was so fun to just show up with him and surprise everybody.

Heavenly Father has blessed us with the knowledge that there is another child that will join our family. We are not sure when or how yet, but we are so happy to know that we will be blessed with more.

Each one of my children has added something wonderful to my life. Jonah has taught me patience and the true meaning of being sympathetic. He is such a strong spirit that needs to be held and loved. Simon has taught me the importance of being happy and having fun. He is the clown of our family and can always make me laugh with either his antics or just his contagious laugh. Luke has taught me love. I never knew that one small child could carry as much love in him as Luke does. And he gives the best hugs.

In turn, each of their birth moms has taught me something equally important—that complete unselfishness and true love go beyond oneself. What wonderful people birth parents are. Without them, I would not have my family. They hold such a special place in my heart!

Chelsea

The Phone Finally Rang!

The Gift of Life

I didn't give you the gift of life,
But in my heart I know.
The love I feel is deep and real,
As if it had been so.

For us to have each other
Is like a dream come true!
No, I didn't give you
The gift of life,
Life gave me the gift of you.

Unknown

    As I was growing up I had the same goals and dreams of most young girls. I always knew that I would grow up, get married, and have children. A family of my own. It's what I wanted more than any other thing. Well, things began to follow in that order. I grew up, got married, and then came the sad reality that we would not be able to move on to that next important step. The children did not come to us in a natural process, as we had assumed that they would.

All of our friends and family members were welcoming new babies into their lives and I could see how happy they were. I longed for the same blessing for us. It was a lonely and helpless feeling. I felt an emptiness that nothing could adequately fill. I was happy for other people as their families began to grow, but I began to feel uncomfortable around them because it made my aching seem harder to bear. I would watch them enjoying what I did not have and what I wanted so desperately. I cried myself to sleep night after night. I prayed to the Lord continually for the blessing of children in my life. My maternal instincts were hard to ignore, and I couldn't understand why I was being denied this choicest blessing that I had looked forward to all of my life. As the years passed, my sadness grew as I was not able to realize the beautiful dream of motherhood and family life. Of course, we pursued all avenues available to us. A long, expensive, and unsuccessful series of infertility treatments. Nothing helped us reach our goal and hope of having a child of our own.

We were always very prayerful during this time, pleading with the Lord for guidance and an answer to our prayers. We made the decision to look into adoption. Our belief was that if we weren't able to get our children to us the natural way, we still wanted them to come! We believed that the Lord would arrange how and whom he chose for us, as he did for all other families. He would just have to make special arrangements in our case. Although I was disappointed at the thought of not being able to bear children, I was more concerned in caring for and loving the children and feeling the joy of being a family. We wanted the experience of having a child of our own and we never worried that we couldn't love an adopted child as our own.

We knew we had so much love to share and we were more than ready to accept the responsibility and blessing of parenting. We knew that a baby was the missing piece that would fill the empty void in our lives and hearts. The days, months, and years seemed to pass so slowly as we waited for and anticipated a child of our own. We knew that it would be such a blessing to us and change and improve our lives in such a profound way . . . and we wanted that! As we were filling out the necessary paperwork for adoption, we had the opportunity to select a preference of boy or girl. We chose "No Preference" because we believed that Heavenly Father was the one who knew who are children were and who was supposed to come to our family, and we wanted him to send the children intended for us. We believed that there was a divine plan for our family, just the same as anyone else's. We couldn't wait to meet our children, to love them and to share our lives with them.

My time and the Lord's due time were not always on the same time table. I wondered if I would ever receive an answer to my prayers and feel the fulfillment of being a mother.

I had a nursery ready and waiting for years. I would walk in there often and dream of the day that a real, little person would occupy that space. I used to look at the crib and rocking chair longingly and then cry at the empty feeling that was a constant ache in my heart. Each time the phone would ring, my hopes would rise, thinking it would be *the* phone call that we were waiting for! With each month that ended, I wondered if I would see another one pass with no word.

Well, *the* phone call did finally come, and on a day that I didn't expect it. I had been feeling sad earlier that day and feeling that I might be childless forever! When the phone rang, I didn't even feel like answering it or talking to anyone so I just let it ring. This was in the days before caller ID. About twenty or so minutes later it rang again. This time I decided that I should answer it and when I did, I was shocked and thrilled beyond description! It was LDS Family Services and immediately my hopes were sky high! I asked, "Are you calling to tell us that you have a baby for us?!" They replied that they needed to talk to both my husband and I. I told them that he was at work. (This was also before the days of cell phones.) I repeated my original question. They told me that I would need to go and contact my husband and call them back when we could both be on the phone together. I said that I would. I again asked if they were calling about a baby. They felt my urgency to know and answered "Yes, it is a about a baby." I let out a cheer of happiness (and relief) and did an excited dance of celebration. Immediately I said, "Is it a boy or a girl?" They said that they couldn't give me any more information until they had both of us on the phone. I was afraid to hang up. I wanted more information. I wanted it to be *real*! I hung up and immediately voiced my gratitude to the Lord as I ran around in no particular direction, feeling like I would burst with excitement and happiness.

At that time, my husband worked construction and was not in an office or near a phone. I knew he could be in a number of different places. I called his work office and they were able to contact him by radio and tell him that he was needed at home immediately. He didn't know what to think and hurried home, worrying that something bad had happened. I could see that by the look on his face, he didn't know what to expect. I was relieved to see him and could barely talk clearly or slowly enough to be understood. I hugged him and said, "We have a baby!" I explained what I knew and we called them back. My initial joy was doubled when we were told that we had a brand new baby daughter! They said that she was healthy, that everything was in order, and that we could pick her up in the morning.

It was a several-hour drive for us. I wanted to see her right away! I could barely contain my enthusiasm. I was happy, relieved, grateful, and anxious all at the same time. I barely slept at all that night and was up bright and early to meet my baby girl. I was ready hours before it was time to go. We passed the time by going shopping for things we thought that we would need. Although we had waited for years for this to happen, we really only had a short time to prepare for the actual event. I remember picking out a special blanket and outfit to bring her home in. Oh the thought of that brought such a spirit of peace, gratitude, and comfort to my heart—a long-awaited answer to our many prayers.

We still ended up arriving early to the agency and I was so anxious to see our baby. We first had to sign some final paperwork and I honestly cannot remember a single word that they said until they stood up and said "Are you ready to meet your daughter?" I began to cry at just the sound of it. They led us down a hallway to a closed door. They opened it, and I could see a frilly bassinet and knew that she was in there. Not because I could visibly see her, but because I could *feel* her! When they opened that door I was surprised to feel a distinct and very familiar spirit! I immediately recognized it as the same spirit that I had felt many times when I was sad and grieving with the pain of being childless. Without being aware of someone being there to give me comfort, I was now experiencing this very familiar spirit present in the room, and realized that it was the spirit of this little child—*my* child! I could barely see what she looked like because of the amount of tears filling my eyes. When I picked her up, she was the most beautiful thing that I had ever seen and my arms and heart that had been empty for so long were now filled with the most precious gift and blessing that I had ever received. My joy and gratitude were overflowing. I felt complete. I was finally a mother!

Jona Webb

Rainbows

We witness a miracle every time a child enters into life.
But those who make their journey home across time and miles,
Growing within the hearts of those who wait to love them,
Are carried on the wings of destiny and placed by God's own hands.

—Kristi Larson

How appropriate, God's promise to us. The rainbow. Filled with beautiful colors. Colors that capture our eye and our heart. What a magnificent thing he chose to remind us of his love for us all. Rainbows are what brought the Marchionna family to the adoption journey.

My husband, David, lost both of his parents within a year of each other. We could do nothing more than look up to the Savior for comfort as we searched for answers. By springtime God was slowly unfolding his plan for us.

It was a cold November evening and the Internet was finally coming into our house. As the new computer was hooked up Ben and Elliot anxiously awaited to be the first to explore its capabilities. My husband had barely stood up before two little bodies slid into his place! I could hear the excitement from the kitchen. I had to go and see what this new technology could do!

I found myself pulling up a chair and inching my way in where all the excitement was. Of course the boys were completely at ease with their new toy. They had gone into search mode. Rainbows were on my scientific boys' minds. The lists and sites were incredible. We all glossed over the words, scanning them quickly as though on a mission! RainbowKids.com sounded interesting. We clicked and then it was coming through. Agencies, countries, and ages were the subtitles. The subtitle "age" jumped out at us. Another click led us to a long listing of children, all by chronological age. We scrolled down to the 5s and clicked, and then a little girl came across the top of the screen. "Sveta B., March 3, 1995" was all we could look at for what seemed an eternity. Then her precious face came clearly across the screen as well as a city called "Ultralsk, Kazakhstan." Little did we know that from this moment we would be forever changed.

Her big, beautiful blue eyes and precious little face captured my heart. Goose bumps, tears of joy, and a feeling of completeness filled my soul. Not only was my heart touched but also David and the boys. The boys shouted, "Let's adopt her!" and as I looked at David, his eyes filled with tears that soon rolled down his cheeks. I knew in an instant that this was what we were to use David's inheritance for. As I recall this event that took place that was so miraculous, so fulfilling I know that only God could have orchestrated it.

Just six months later we had moved into a bigger home and were now in Kazakhstan, anxiously waiting to meet our daughter Sveta.

We were allowed to keep Sveta from 10 AM to 6 PM for four days. During those four days I really felt like we were a family. One of Sveta's favorite things to do was to take a bath—she is just like her brothers and loves water. "Mama, Papa, smaltree," (Mama, Papa, look at me) she would say while lying quietly on the bottom of the tub. The warm, bubbly water covered every part of her body except for her little face. Her eyes were closed as she floated, waving her arms. Tears filled our eyes as I couldn't help but wonder what was going through her mind. Her little body was so at peace, fulfilled with her dream of finally having a family.

As I would gently lie next to her on the bed in our hotel room, Sveta's body would just melt into mine. I can't tell you how many times she would look up at me and smile. It was as though she couldn't believe her dreams had come true. "Moya, Mama," Sveta would softly speak.

Through this journey I have learned and realized that all things are possible! God will make a way, when there seems to be *no* way. He works in ways we cannot see; he made a way for me! God guided me on this road to Sveta. Thank you, Lord.

Liliya

I must share the arrival of our daughter Liliya.

The agency we went through for Sveta was called "Tree of Life Agency." They had over-nighted a video of Sveta and some other children in the orphanage. We had found another child that we wanted to adopt along with Sveta. Upon arriving in Kazakhstan we were informed that the birth mother for this other child had backed out at the last minute. Feeling strongly that we needed to find a sister for Sveta, we asked the orphanage to find a suitable girl.

Our relationship with Liliya's caretakers was not as close as the one we had with Sveta's. The baby orphanage was run very differently. Our conversations and interactions were limited because of the protective rules during visitation. However, you would not have known this on the day we arrived to bring Liliya home.

We were happily greeted by a slew of looks. We were escorted by six women, three of whom wore white doctor coats; the other three were nicely dressed. We entered a room that looked like a music room. A piano was in the corner along with two rows of benches. Beautiful lace curtains covered the windows. On the right of us there appeared to be a large puppet theatre layed against a drab white wall. While we anxiously awaited Liliya's arrival, we made small talk with our translator Kinkush. Elliot and Ben were fighting over who would hold Sveta. I laughed to myself as I watched Sveta find a seat for herself.

As the door gently creaked open, a kind doctor entered. Her face and words seemed familiar to me. She spoke few English words, only enough to get her point across. I loved her dark bobbed hair; it framed her smiley face perfectly. Soon everyone was in the room; the doctor took a seat at a desk in front of us. Seven other teachers and nurses filled the benches behind us.

Finally the moment we had all been waiting for, Liliya walked proudly into the room. She looked like a little angel. Dave and I moved down onto the floor so she could see us with ease. Our eyes met, I could hear her teachers call out, "Liliya, your mama and papa." I was silent as her petite legs carried her quickly into my arms. Liliya wasted no time kissing all of us. Ben, Elliot, and Sveta were all in line for their kisses too.

We all moved back to the tiny wooden benches so that the doctors could speak. Irene began her speech with tears in her eyes. She recalled that yesterday in the courtroom she realized we were a family that loved the Lord and relied on our faith to carry us through life. She knew that faith would help us in the future. Dave and I gripped one another's hands tighter. I was fighting tears again. We signed Liliya's shop records and Irene reached out to hug us.

Kinkush, our translator, told us they would like me to say a few words. *Oh no,* I thought, as I slowly walked toward the front of the room. My mind raced diligently thinking of what to say. Liliya gripped my neck tighter as I turned to face the row of anxious listeners. My good-bye speech began with credits to my Heavenly Father as he had truly brought us together and completed us as a family. As I shared my heartfelt feelings, my emotions began to overflow. The words came from my lips, and the tears streamed down the faces of my listeners. I reassured them that Dave and I would rely on our faith to guide our family. I spoke of Dave's love for the girls and the boys' love of having sisters. As my final words were said, we all wiped the tears from our eyes; then we hugged and kissed. Liliya's caretakers gave the final farewell and quickly walked from the room. Our time there was precious. I will never forget that day. One day we will relive it as we tell our sweet little Liliya her story.

As Dave and I lay quietly next to each other that night replaying in our minds the amazing events that had taken place, each of us thanked God for completing our family, Dave leaned over, kissed my forehead, and said, "Bethann, we just tucked in our whole family: our two sons and our two daughters. This is truly a dream come true." As I propped myself up, I just gazed at them and felt such great love for all of my sleeping children. With the overwhelming love that I knew God had for me and his children, a feeling overcame me that someday I would be back in Kazakhstan.

During our four-week life-changing stay in Uralsk, Kazakhstan, many rainbows danced across the sky!

Bethann Marchionna in the orphanage in Uralsk, Kazakhstan.

Every child born into the world is a new thought of God,
An ever fresh radiant possibility

—Kate Douglas Wiggin

Joel

 The fields have surely been plowed and seeds have been planted on behalf of the many orphan children of Uralsk. Seeing how God is truly mindful of the fatherless and the disabled has really touched my heart.

 The plowing began in 2004 when my friend Lilya and I travelled to explore the possibilities of working within the orphanages. I had no idea that what would happen on this journey would change my family again and drive me to my knees to deal with my greatest fears.

 While in Kushum Orphanage for Disabled Children, a charismatic fourteen-year-old boy by the name of Amazhol was brought into my life. He was afflicted with Klippel-Treanuany-Weber Syndrome. My heart ached as we left and I promised to find a mama and papa for him. Upon my returning home, my friends and family prayed constantly on his behalf. A desire crept into my heart like a spark and the flame grew until I could not put the fire out. I wrestled with the Lord and begged Him to take this desire away. It didn't make any earthly sense; first and foremost we had no money! Second, we had no room, and third our oldest boys were upset with the idea and struggled to come to terms with another sibling. I told no one about the struggle within me, but the Lord just kept nudging me forward.

 One night I had the most realistic dream. I was in labor and I was in so much pain. David was at my side gently encouraging me with his kind words. As I began to push I struggled and struggled. The staff was encouraging me to keep up the good work: "You're almost there, you can do it!" The unusual part was that I had never had a vaginal birth. I had had two c-sections. As I continued to work hard to bring this baby into life, I looked down and could see the baby's head. I reached down to grab the baby and lifted him to me, and looking straight at me with his big brown eyes and black hair, it was Joel. As I lifted him to my chest I notice his left leg was enlarged. I wept. When I awoke I found my back was drenched with sweat and my stomach muscles ached as if I had just done a hundred sit-ups. What had happened? I woke David and shared with him what had just happened, explaining that we had been chosen by God to adopt Amanzhol. David quickly responded with "I know Bethann."

I fell to my knees and poured out my heart in prayer with many questions. My answer came with the thought "Just step out. With man, Bethann, this is impossible, but with God all things are possible"

So with the many obstacles we had to overcome the Lord was continually showing his wondrous hand in all of this. Once again on October 12 we arrived in Uralsk, Kazakhstan, eagerly waiting to see Joel. The girls and I went to the Ministry of Education office to get permission to go and see Joel. We sat before three people who asked us questions such as: "Why are you doing this?" And, "Do you receive money from your government for adopting?" They asked the girls if they liked living in the United States and if they liked their family. After a lot of grueling, we were finally given permission to see Joel. A kind Kazak women escorted us to the village where Joel anxiously waited.

We drove through the crater-filled dirt road with careful precision as our driver maneuvered toward a blue and white orphanage where Joel was waiting. To my surprise as the large gate swung open Joel was standing right in its entrance! I jumped to the edge of my seat as the girls shouted "There he is!" The van door slid open and I leapt out and raced toward Joel. "Mama," he exclaimed as our arms wrapped around one another. I lifted his feet up off the ground and I could hear laughter behind me as Joel tucked his head on my shoulder. I just kept his body lifted in my arms! Sveta, Liliya, and our interpreter came quickly to our side as we all hugged. Joel kept looking up at me with a smile that you can't imagine. I could see the wonderment in his eyes and his thoughts were coming through his eyes. "I can't believe it. They are here, and I am holding my *mother*."

There are no words that can describe his facial expression. I try to imagine the yearning in his heart for the past sixteen years to know the love of a father and mother. While we were there Joel was asked by the director to sing his song about mothers. As Joel glanced over with a look of anticipation he nodded "yes." He reached over and held my hand as he began to sing his song with such heartfelt expression about mothers. It was then that I felt that Lord just come down and sit in the room! There was not a dry tear that room.

Finally it was time for us to leave. I could see Joel's face showing a look of bravery as he prepared to release me for one more day. As we all emotionally said good-bye, Joel glanced into my eyes like a scared puppy before he launched into my arms. I held him tightly and whispered in his ear, "Thank you God." He responded in a choked up voice, "Da, Mama, da."

Our adoption process went extremely well. It was over quickly and we were granted our son. As we entered the hall, Joel's big eyes looked up at us. We stretched forth our arms, and said "Joel Marchionna, our son, come here." Joel jumped from his seat as he shouted "Slava Bagoo," (Praise the Lord).

As I look back over these miraculous events I can see how God had been preparing me. Even though my spirit fought the will of God with my selfish thoughts and fears. The Lord knew how to change my heart and mind. I cannot thank the Lord enough for all his love for me and my family. May God ignite your faith as you read our story.

Proverbs 3:5–6 reads "Trust in the Lord with all thine heart, and lean not unto thine own understanding, but in all thy ways acknowledge him and he shall direct thy paths." I hope that you will believe him and the great plans he has for all of us.

Bethann Marchionna

My Sweet M&M

*And whoever welcomes a little child like this
in my name welcomes me.*
Matthew 18:5

About five years ago we were meandering through life totally content and happy. We had been blessed with three beautiful biological children ages nine, eleven, and thirteen at the time. I guess God perhaps smiled upon us and thought, their lives seem to be running smoothly, perhaps they're up for a bit of a challenge. So the whole process began. First we began to notice little children wherever we'd go and talk about how much we missed our kids being little again. Then my husband began to talk about how wonderful it would be to make a difference in the life of a child that really needed a loving home. He didn't care how it happened; his heart is just always open to helping and loving those in need.

It didn't take long for God to start working on me too and after a series of inspirations and miracles, I knew that we needed to help children whose lives had been somewhat broken. My heart and mind were immediately turned to the foster care program in our state. We first however, had to get our older children on board. All three of them are great with younger kids and babies.

My husband and I both had served missions for our church and were consistently teaching our children of the joyous opportunity of serving others. We approached it by calling it a mini mission for our family. We would serve children who were in need in our community, and whatever the outcome we all had to be on board. So they prayed about it and we all agreed.

Our time in foster care was a wonderful experience for us all. First came a baby boy, who made us all smile instantly with the sweetest disposition you've ever seen. The kids loved bathing and dressing him, because he smiled no matter what you were doing with him. He returned home after a couple of months.

We then had our first experience with a sibling group. This interested us because we couldn't bear the thought of siblings being split apart after already being removed from their parents. These cute sisters were three and five. They missed home so badly and needed love and assurance that all would be well. They stayed with us for three months. Everyone always asks if it is difficult to send a child home to less-than-favorable circumstances should the courts return them. My answer is always a little mixed. You miss the child but are thankful for whatever time you could provide a warm loving environment. The rest I tried to leave in God's hands. In our case most of the families that received second chances tried to better their lives for the sake of their children. I loved and admired the families we worked with, even with all the problems they were battling. I prayed for them each day along with their children. I believe God forgives and gives opportunities for people to change.

By opening myself up to loving in this way I found it to be a most rewarding experience. In the fall of 2003 we received a call asking us to take a brother and sister. Miguel was two and his sister Mikayla was only one at the time. They had been placed with family members for about ten months but were being placed back into the foster care system due to some threats made by their birth mom. The extended family hoped for an unrelated adoptive family. This would provide a safe home and growing up experience for the kids.

We were selected and could hardly wait for them to arrive. They were both the most beautiful babies. (Okay, they weren't babies, but remember my "baby" was nearly ten.) We instantly fell in love with them. Amazingly enough, within two months after they arrived, their birth mom relinquished her rights. The birth dad was already out of the picture. It took nine months to finalize our adoption (kind of like a pregnancy term).

Our adoption experience has been challenging but more rewarding than anything we've ever done. We love having a larger family even amidst the chaos at times. (We often joke that we have no time for midlife crises because we're too busy to schedule one in.) A loving Father in Heaven orchestrated all of this and our lives have all been changed for the better as a result.

 Tracy Larsen

Love Is Love!

Biology is the least of what makes someone a mother.

—Oprah Whinfrey

Though adoption was not what I had envisioned happening in my life, I'm grateful for it as it has allowed me to love and parent two of my three children. I also had the opportunity to have a biological child as well, and the love is the same. Children are children, and love is love—I have never felt there was a difference. While it is a wonderful experience to carry and give birth to a child, it's also a wonderful experience to give love and care to a child who's been given life by another.

I can remember the exact moment when I first felt love for each of my children. For Rebecca it was during her first doctor's appointment while they were weighing her. She was crying and they told me to pick her up as they had finished weighing and measuring her. As I hugged her close to me, I had a sudden feeling of great love for her. She was my daughter! With Tyler it was when we returned home after going to the hospital with an appendicitis attack with my husband, James. My sister had come to tend Rebecca and Tyler while we were gone and when I walked in the door and said to my kids "Mama's home," I felt a great love for Tyler, and knew he was my son. With Michael it was when they laid him in my arms after he was delivered and I saw the little baby I'd been carrying within me for nine months. They all came as little strangers needing my love and care; in giving that love and care, it returned to me tenfold.

I anticipated that the court proceedings of the adoption would be some legality that had to happen—something businesslike and cold. What a surprise to find it was neither. While we did have to prove we were fit to be parents for our children, it was awe-inspiring to hear the judge tell us that we were to consider this little baby our child in every sense of the word. She would need our physical, emotional, and financial help throughout her life. In many ways I felt cheated to not be able to take our youngest child to court—he was simply born to us and we didn't have to prove to anyone our ability to parent him. The legal reminders of what parents do in raising children were some of the best memories I have. I remember loving both my children even more after the adoption proceedings.

I told my children early on that they were adopted. I didn't want it to be something secret—or something I would keep to myself until a certain age when I would then blow their minds with the information. I've been honest and open with them when they've asked about their birth parents and the circumstances that brought them to me.

I remember my son, Tyler, telling me how he told his friends that he was adopted and about his "real mom." He told me that he meant the mom who gave birth to him. I then asked him if I looked fake to him. "Mom," he said, rolling his eyes, "you know what I mean." I told him I understood his meaning but I also wanted him to understand mine. I said, "I know I didn't give birth to you but I have been your mom in every way since the day you were a day old so don't tell me I'm not your 'real mom.'"

I would wholeheartedly recommend adoption to couples seeking to have children.

Lynne Holly

Our Road to Adoption

And he took a child, and set him in the midst of them: and when he had taken him in his arms, he said unto them, Whosoever shall receive one of such children in my name, receiveth me: and whosoever shall recieve me, receiveth not me, but him that sent me.
St Mark 9:36–37

Part I

    I have always been a "late-bloomer" as my mom used to call me. The youngest in my class, I was the last to do so many things. I also was delayed in figuring out my career path and very late in finding the love of my life to settle down to get married. When I finally did, I was nearing my mid-thirties and knew that we really should get started on our family shortly after getting married. Luckily for us, I did get pregnant after about a year of marriage. Unluckily for us, I miscarried shortly after our pregnancy test came back positive. Although we were devastated with this loss, we were determined to try again. And that we did: tried and tried and tried. My husband is an airline pilot and we actually have some fond memories of the times I tagged along on his international flights because "the time was right." We tried conceiving in Brussels, London, Puerto Rico, and even at a convent we stayed at to visit my sister in Rome. Some said we could be trying too hard—that perhaps stress was preventing us from succeeding. I even quit my successful job at a company for which I had worked for over fourteen years, just to make sure that the stress factor wasn't working against us.

While I was still at that job, however, I had hired a young assistant who shared with me the joy she felt in volunteering at a crisis nursery center. I immediately looked in to that opportunity and I, too, began to feel that joy. I spent every Monday night for the next couple of years holding, feeding, bathing, and loving kids who had been taken from their parents or had been left there by parents who realized they couldn't handle the daunting task of parenting. This helped me to deal with our inability to get pregnant, despite all the infertility support we had undergone.

I always left the crisis nursery with mixed emotions. I was so sad at the thought of all those kids needing good homes, yet so happy that I could make them feel wanted and loved, even for a couple of hours. After each night there, I would go home and tell my husband about each child that had touched me and tell him how hard it was to leave, knowing the trauma that their little psyches must be enduring. One night after hearing my stories and my comment about, "Those poor little things, waiting for a home and someone to love them . . ." my husband surprised me with his response: "Let's take one." My jaw could have hit the floor. You see, my husband had always been very opposed to even a suggestion that we look into adoption. I was heartbroken at his resistance to adoption, but this idea gave me a renewed sense of hope. We talked about it more, and the next day I began the research to see what being a foster parent would entail.

Actually, the foster licensing process was a healthy and welcomed diversion to our infertility challenges. We really enjoyed taking the classes that were required to be licensed and although those classes contained many cautions about being a foster parent in an attempt to adopt, we were intrepid about forging ahead to "rescue" a young one who needed a home.

Once our classes were completed we were eligible to take in a child. Our licensing worker warned me not to try to "pick out" our own foster child when I went to the crisis nursery center. She said there were lots of options of where our first placement would come from, and that we might not have any control of where that might be. Regardless, I will always have a vivid memory of the night I held a sweet little Hispanic baby who was pretty distraught and had a hard time going to sleep. Every time I'd get him calmed down and sleeping, I would go to put him in his crib and he would awaken and cry again. I returned to the rocking chair with him and started the whole process over again. After a good two hours of this routine, I finally was successful in getting him to bed (although I had stayed two extra hours to do so!). Before I left, I asked some of the workers at the center if they knew if that little guy was waiting for a foster home. They looked at his chart, and I knew they knew the answer to my question, but they responded that they really couldn't reveal that information to me. I told them that my husband and I had just gotten our foster license and that I sure wished I could take that one. (I knew I had been warned about this, but I just couldn't help myself!)

Two days later, I got a call from our licensing worker. Her first comment was that she had a potential placement for us, and she kind of wondered if I might know the baby whom she had in mind. She told me his birth date, his current location—which was the crisis shelter—and his name. My heart started to pound and a smile spread across my face. Yes, indeed, I did know the little guy. It was the one I had rocked to sleep so many times two nights earlier. The next step was to introduce my husband to him and then we would be able to determine if the placement was a good fit for us.

Later that day I returned to the crisis center with my husband. It was fun to see him interact with all those kids and I knew immediately that he recognized my passion for going there once a week. They brought the little guy to us shortly after we arrived and the worker put him in my arms. It was like he recognized me because he immediately smiled as I snuggled him against me. The rush of joy I felt was short-lived as my husband took him away from me and started to coo and gurgle and do all the sappy things that baby lovers do to show their instantaneous affection for the adorable bundles of joy. There was no question that we would be taking that baby home with us. We made the call right then and there to our licensing worker to let her know of our intent.

The next couple of days were a whirlwind as we shopped and researched for all the things one would need to take care of a four-month-old baby. No baby showers for us. We loaded a cart at Target and a baby store and actually bought the car seat on our way back to the center two days later to pick up the sweet boy. We had visitors that very day coming to see our addition. Everyone fell in love with him immediately. That night I hardly slept, just taking in the sounds and the smells of his being in our home. In the morning as my husband carried him down the stairs, he looked at me and said, "This one I could keep!" I couldn't believe my ears. This baby had stolen my husband's heart after less than twenty-four hours in our home.

There was such a purpose in our lives and we adapted very easily to parenting, even when it meant rushing him to an emergency room because he had been sick and started wheezing to the degree that he couldn't get enough air. The many days that followed with giving breathing treatments and medication to clear his lungs from the terrible virus he had contracted just seemed like a "do what you need to do" task and never seemed to daunt us.

Months passed, the birth mom showed up for her first scheduled visit with him and then never came again. It amazed me to think of how anyone could be apathetic about such a loveable little guy, but it was evident early on that the relationship we were developing with our foster son had the potential to be a permanent one. Eighteen months later, we spent my fortieth birthday in a courtroom, surrounded by family and friends as we adopted that "little guy." He's now ten-and-a-half and is still the light of our life—or one of the lights, I should say. Lucky for us . . .

Part II

Once our adoption was finalized, what I call the "rescue factor" soon set in—really soon. Ten days later, I received another call from our licensing worker. There was a little girl at another area crisis center that needed a home. She was just a bit over a year old, I was told. I thought another little angel in the house would be so good for all of us and I wasted no time in scooping up our little guy, then twenty-two months old, and taking him with me to go visit this little sweetie. On the way there, we practiced saying her name and decided to use a shortened version as the full name was too hard to pronounce for our novice talker. It was an unusually rainy day and I was actually glad for the activity of a nice drive in the drizzle and rain. Just as we were turning the last corner before we arrived at the crisis center, I looked ahead and saw a giant double rainbow which

I pointed out to my son. "This is a sign from God," I thought. "This little girl will bring a beautiful light to our life."

When we arrived at the center, the workers thoughtfully had all the other kids leave the common area, so that we could have some quality time with our potential foster child. I couldn't believe how incredibly sweet she was—such a petite little body, a round angel face, and a mop of curly hair that made her look more like she was twelve than one. Sadly, though, there was not much life in her eyes. She looked at us, but it didn't seem like she really saw us, more like she was looking through us. I was determined to make her smile. I find it very easy to be affectionate with kids, so I caressed her little arms and stroked her curls. She soon warmed up to me and loosened up. I gave her some gentle tickles, and then the sweet smiles appeared. Still, she was not very willing to play, especially not with her potential brother. It was early evening, and I knew the routines of crisis centers, so I asked if it might be time for her to take a bath. It was, and they let me do the honors. I loved seeing that little sweetie splash in the big sink where we bathed her. I couldn't wait to lavish those curls with bubbles and see the drips of water clump the long eyelashes that adorned her cherub face. She loved her bath and I loved cuddling her in the warm thick towel before we dressed this little doll in her jammies. Despite the little something about the look—or maybe it was the absence of the look in her eyes—I decided we would take her. Lucky for me, my husband trusted my intuition about the right thing to do, and even though he was out of town on a trip, I let our licensing worker know that we would take this sweetheart into our home.

The next day, our worker called again to complete the arrangements. She commented that she was a bit surprised that we were taking her because she was so close in age to our son. I responded that I thought she was about thirteen or fourteen months old, but that I actually had not heard her birth date. Turns out that she was only five weeks younger than our son, and the appearance of her being much younger may have been due to developmental delay. For a short period, I had a pang of regret, wondering if this would be the right thing to do for our family. I discussed it with my husband, and he assured me that if she needed a good home, her age did not matter. I must say that I was a bit reluctant as we made arrangements to pick her up.

This was the first time that my husband laid eyes on this sweetheart. She was all "dolled up" in a pretty purple dress with a big ribbon holding her curls away from her eyes on top of her head. She seemed to be so scared of this big man whom she had never seen before. However, she easily reached out for me and let me put her in our car. My husband commented about her eyes and the lack of contact. I told him she just needed some love to brighten up.

We left the center and went right to my parents' house to celebrate my dad's seventy-sixth birthday. We surprised my whole family as we walked in with another child. They all loved her instantly, and she was passed around to all my sisters who snuggled and loved her upon taking her in their arms. She ate like a she was on a mission, especially the cake and ice cream. I've never seen a little one take to ice cream with such a vengeance! She seemed like she was in heaven, and the smiles finally came. I think that might have been my dad's favorite birthday gift that year—our little sweetheart, who brought such smiles to his face on that September 16.

The next few weeks presented more challenges than we anticipated as this little sweetie tried to adjust to a normal home. She was hard to read, hard to please, and *very* hard to pacify. All of the maternal urges and methods that had worked so successfully with our first were to no avail in caring for this one. Stroking, snuggling, soothing, and assuring . . . none of them had a positive effect as this little one spent much of her time screaming at any sense of discomfort. There were too many nights where she awakened in terror and was unable to calm down, despite efforts by my husband or me. We had a new case manager from the agency who should have given us more information about her background and helped to equip us to provide for her special needs. Turns out there was much more baggage that this sweetheart came with than we had ever anticipated could come with a twenty-one month old little girl. Suffice it to say, this one was so hard to care for.

By this time my dad's health had taken a bad turn and we spent months visiting him in the hospital. Some of those visits were actually respite time for me to take a break from this little one who had no skills to cope with everyday discomforts. My dad actually was unable to talk because of a trach tube they had to put in to allow him to breathe. After months of struggles at home and enduring the stress of my dad's declining health, my husband and I decided that it would be best to move this little sweetheart to another home, one where the parents might be better equipped to deal with her emotional outbursts and struggles. I'll never forget the day I broke this news to Dad as he lay in his hospital bed. He had loved her so much and I knew it would be hard for him to understand our decision. When I finally got the words out between my tears, he simply looked in my eyes and with heartfelt support he mouthed these words to me, "Let Jesus take care of it."

I finally came to my spiritual senses and took his advice to heart. Even though we had discussed our resolve to pass her on, we never again took any initiative to make it happen. A couple of days later, we got a call that our caseworker had been fired and the new one provided so much support and advice about caring for our foster daughter. We took an awesome class she recommended and became so much more informed about the emotional and developmental challenges of children who suffer from attachment disorders. We were encouraged by a respected child psychologist that with consistent love and a good home environment, this sweetheart could make the turn and become emotionally stronger and normal.

Sadly, my dad passed away a few months later. But after he did, this sweetheart was able to sleep at night, never again awakening in inconsolable terror. She now had an angel with her at night—the one who reminded me to let Jesus take care of it.

This foster case had a much longer road in terms of finality and red tape. But as God would have it, two and a half years later, we were again in a courtroom, surrounded with family, (minus Dad) joyously and legally making this sweetheart, *our* sweetheart. She is now ten and a half as well and although she shows some developmental learning challenges and still has quite a feisty streak, our daughter is a sparkler in our lives and we love how she still challenges us to stay on our toes to provide direction for her.

Part III

Less than a month after we adopted our daughter, still another call came from our licensing worker. Keep in mind that it had been an exhausting road providing for her emotional challenges and dealing with the death of my Dad was taking its toll on me emotionally. As I listened to the words of the worker, "no, no, no" kept popping in my head. She was describing a baby boy who had been born with several drugs in his system. He had gone through a month of detox in the hospital, and had been in a group home for the past two months. He was having real physical struggles due to his prenatal drug exposure and was quite irritable and physically uncomfortable on an ongoing basis. The worker told me she thought of me because I was a stay-at-home mom and they were requesting a stable environment to try to calm his disposition. I mentally fought with the notion of taking another irritable and difficult baby into our home. I was tired and drained and honestly felt that ours would not be the best home for such a child, but slightly, ever so slightly, I felt that "rescue tug" pulling at my heartstrings. I'm not quite sure why I asked for his birth date. Maybe it was because we had been mislead about the actual age of our daughter before we agreed to take her. As soon as I heard the answer, that "tug" became a yank! This little guy had been born on September 16, the same birthday as my dad. Without making a commitment, I asked if perhaps I could just meet this one, somehow, in honor of my dad.

I got directions to the group home and debated with myself about if I should take the other two children with me. After all, I wasn't going to take this one, and I didn't want to confuse them about why we were going to see a baby. My neighbor generously offered to take the kids, even though she had three young ones of her own. I dropped them off and started on my way, wondering why I was even doing this! On the way, it began to rain really hard and I turned on my wipers. They were so sun damaged that they didn't even work and I could barely see through the windshield. I decided that it was a sign that I really shouldn't make this trek. I called my neighbor to say that I was coming back for the kids due to the rain. She talked me out of changing my plans, even offering for me to take her car. (I guess I also could have stopped for some wipers, but that would have been too easy!) Instead, due to her insistence that I go see this baby, I stopped at the repair shop where my husband had dropped his car before he left to go out of town. They had just finished repairing it, so I left my car there and jumped in his to finish my trek. I still was questioning why I was going through these motions, when I clearly didn't think that this baby was a good fit for our family right now.

When I arrived at the group home, the workers were friendly, but apprehensive about bringing out this baby. I braced myself for a screamer, but didn't hear any sounds at all as they approached me with the little bundle. As I sat in a chair, the apprehensive face of the worker turned up into a smile, the kind that is part smile, part pride. She laid him in my lap. What I was looking at was one of the most beautiful sights I have ever seen. This ever-so-sweet baby, with dark flawless skin and deep large brown eyes, looked up at me intently and smiled the biggest, most precious smile, so big and beautiful, flashing those new-baby gums and sporting just one deep dimple on his left cheek. As I cooed and awwed and took in the lovely sight of him, he only smiled and squealed more intensely. He stole my heart, this precious September 16 baby. I asked a few more questions and was told that he had actually been extremely sick the past few days and was being seen by a doctor that day. He had a terrible virus that had affected his respiratory system and he had nausea and diarrhea as well. I was so surprised to hear this—if this smiling little bundle was sick, what would his temperament be like when he was well? I saw absolutely no signs of the irritability that had been described by my licensing worker. The gal at the group home said that when he came he was quite distressed for several days, but all of the workers there had fallen in love with him and held him around the clock, trying to ease his discomfort. Their diligence had paid off because this little guy was nothing but sweet! All of the workers there had become so attached that they were sad to know that they were now looking for a foster/adoption home for him, hence the apprehension in bringing him out for me to see. (It was fairly certain that this case would go right to adoption as the history of this baby's family warranted it.)

    I called my husband on his cell phone. When he answered I said, "I'm holding a really precious little boy and he needs a home. I think we should take another." He laughed his deep belly laugh, knowing that I was 100 percent serious and how his role in taking in our kids was always diminished by his being out of town. He has often joked throughout our marriage that I "drive the boat" and he just "water-skis behind it!" He told me if that was what I wanted, he was just fine with it. I asked if he wanted to meet the baby before I brought him home, and he assured me that he trusted what I was doing and that he would just be ready to come home to a house with three kids instead of two.

    Next I called our licensing worker to tell her that we wanted to take this precious boy. I asked her if I would be able to just take him home with me that day. She had me hand the phone to the staff member in charge and they decided that I should come back the next day after he was released from the doctor's care for the virus he was trying to get over. That actually was a better plan, as I still needed to get baby supplies and pull our crib out of storage. Reluctantly, I had to hand my precious one back to the worker. I apologized that I would have to take him away from them permanently the next day.

On my way home, I called my neighbor and told her the news. She couldn't have been more thrilled for me. I thanked her for encouraging me to go, despite the heavy rain. On the drive back, I knew that I would not see another rainbow through the dreary skies, but I sure felt one in my heart.

The next morning, as I dropped the kids off at preschool, I got another phone call from our licensing worker. She informed me that there had been some miscommunication and that the precious boy that I was planning to pick up later that day had been visited by another couple only a few hours ago and they were preparing to take him home with them that day. My heart sunk! I was so disappointed. It took me a few seconds to think of the words to try to advocate for my case. I told her that I had actually wanted to take him with me the night before and had communicated that to the staff member in charge. She had not allowed me to take him until after he saw a doctor who would release him to move to a private home. Apparently, at this point he had been seen by a doctor and the staff person in charge that day had assumed that the couple who were there at that moment was the same party that had requested to take him the day before. She didn't spend any more time on the phone with me but set out to try to untangle the miscommunication and confusion. My phone rang again a few minutes later, and she informed me that, indeed, because I had made the commitment to take him first, he would be coming to our home. I had a mixed rush of emotions—part ecstasy that he would be with us and part regret for the poor couple who had to receive the bad news that they would not be taking him. I really did feel compassion for them hearing that news and I actually still do. I pondered back on the situation of almost not going the day before because of the rain, and felt so grateful to my neighbor, my friend, for her role in encouraging me to go. If not for her, things would definitely be different.

My next stop was to go to the store to buy diapers, formula, bibs, clothes, even a car seat. As I unloaded my heaping cart onto the conveyor belt, the young cashier must have thought my statement rather odd. "I'm getting a baby today!" I exclaimed proudly.

My sister accompanied me to the group home a few hours later, along with my other two children. We all enjoyed seeing the other kids at the home and in fact, brought along several wrapped gifts for them since it was just a week before Christmas. I loved how my little ones, now just four years old, displayed such joy in giving those gifts and helping the kids unwrap, open, and play with them. But I must say, the real gift was ours, as they brought out our freshly bathed little precious dimpley boy. He quickly stole the hearts of my sister and kids too. After we brought him to our car and buckled him safely in his new car seat, my son said, "Look Mom, I'm blessing him" as he reached over and drew a cross on dimple boy's forehead. What a precious moment.

That night as we ate our dinner, we couldn't bear to not look at this sweet baby, so we put him on the table in his infant seat so we could look at him while we ate. We positioned him at the end of the table, but soon realized that he could come a little closer. My sister jokingly started to sing, "Come a little bit closer, you're my kind of man . . ." to which dimple boy flashed that winning smile and showed us his one dimple. We all giggled and planted that moment in our hearts.

My husband came home a day later and laid eyes on the baby. He was instantly won over! "Good job," he told me. "He's adorable!" My family agreed. We all got together to celebrate my daughter's baptism which happened just two days after the baby came to us. Then two days after that, I loaded three kids, four suitcases, three car seats and a diaper bag into my car and through the airport to meet up with my husband in Dallas, where he had to sit on call over Christmas. It was tricky travelling with three little ones now and I remember just how much that sunk in when we were all buckled in our seats and I had to use the bathroom! Thank heaven for helpful flight attendants who kept an eye on my cherubs so I could have a moment of privacy!

I loved that Christmas, even though we had to be away from our extended families. There was something so meaningful and special about spending the Lord's birthday with our sweet addition to our already sweet family. Of course we prayed for a speedy adoption road for this never irritable little miracle boy, and our prayers were answered. In just over a year, we were back in court, making our family of five a legal reality. As we drove home from the adoption, we were listening to the radio and conversing at the same time. My daughter interrupted our conversation and yelled, "Listen to the song on the radio!" We turned it up to hear that memorable song, "Come a little bit closer, you're my kind of man . . ." How apropos to seal that special day!

Dimple boy now fills our lives with his impish smile every day and every night I aim my lips for that dimple on the left side of his cheek and thank God that he answered our prayers for a family in the most special, miraculous, and faith-directed way. Sometimes we marvel at the irony of how much we had struggled to get pregnant and how serendipitously God provided. By the grace of God, we are blessed with three wonderful children who fill our lives with joys and challenges meant just for us, through God's almighty plan. Lucky for us . . .

Sue Perovich

My Tracey

*I know God won't give me anything I can't handle.
I just wish he didn't trust me so much*

—Mother Teresa

Thirty-seven years ago our second child (and our second daughter) was born. A beautiful baby, she scared the doctor because he noticed she stayed in the fetal position and would not stretch her limbs. Before he told us of his concerns, he called our pediatrician, who came immediately to check the baby. He told us our little Tiffany had a rare condition called arthrogryposis multiplex, a condition manifesting itself with a lower muscle mass throughout the body, creating general weakness. The loss of muscle happens during pregnancy, much like the loss of muscle in muscular dystrophy.

For five years we enjoyed the association of our special little daughter. Tiffany required extensive physical therapy in order to strengthen the muscle tissue remaining in her body. She had surgery to encourage the growth of an inadequate hip socket. When she was close to her first birthday, she had a respiratory arrest following surgery. That event introduced us to one of the symptoms of her condition—weakened lungs, as part of her weak muscular system.

Tiffany was never strong enough to stand alone or to walk. A happy girl, she would scoot around in a sitting position, and look at books, listen to records, and play with her sisters, one older and one younger. By the age of five, Tiffany had experienced several mechanical pneumonias—a result of lungs not strong enough to stay inflated. Finally, her little heart gave up trying to pump blood through collapsed lungs.

Two months after Tiffany passed away, another daughter was born into our family. While she was still a new baby, we as parents decided we wanted to adopt a handicapped child. We felt that we had been blessed to know of the love a special needs child has to give, as well as having learned how to care for such a child and give him or her our love.

We made some phone calls and found only one agency who handled special needs adoptions at that time. They pretty much ignored our inquiries, probably because we had a six-week-old baby. How could such a couple want another new child *now*?

We persisted, and succeeded in having our names put on a national adoption exchange. We indicated an age range, and the types of disabilities we would be willing to consider. Approximately one year later, we were told that it would be a good idea for us to learn sign language. We enrolled in a community school class. Then we were told we could go to Denver to meet a six-year-old little girl who had cerebral palsy. She had been chosen to be our new daughter. Tracey could not talk, but knew some sign language. She walked with braces. We spent a week getting acquainted, and then took her home with us.

Tracey had been adopted at birth by a couple who were not aware of her condition. By the time she was a year old, it became obvious that she was not going to be able to perform the functions of a normal little girl. Her handicap proved to be a hindrance to the marriage relationship of her parents. She was given up to the state at the age of two. From that time until we adopted her, at almost seven years of age, she was cared for in foster homes.

As a young child, Tracey was rarely taken out of the home because of the difficulty of caring for her. Her lack of experience in the real world, we discovered, along with the trauma of moving to a new family, made her physical difficulties very much secondary to her emotional needs. She cried for no apparent reason and would not quit. If we asked a simple question, she would cry because she didn't know what answer we wanted her to give. Questions like, "Would you like more spaghetti?" would create such stress in her mind that she could not handle it. New situations, likewise, brought uncontrollable crying. Everything in life seemed to be beyond her capacity to handle.

Since coming into our family, Tracey has had surgery to help her to walk without braces. She has been well accepted into classes at school and church. Our neighbors have always been helpful and friendly. At first, Tracey attended a special school for disabled children, and then moved on to a normal school with pull-out classes for special needs children. She writes in manuscript form, something we were told that she would never have the ability to do. Tracey still has to be very careful not to fall because she has no natural reflex to reach out and catch herself. Her most obvious physical characteristic is a very large, happy smile that she gives to everyone she meets.

Tracey is now almost thirty-eight years old. She has seven living siblings, all married. Tracey lives at home with her parents and performs several hours per day of data entry (extraction) work as a service to her church. Tracey's keyboarding is performed with one finger on one hand, her only good hand. She works hard and enjoys contributing accurate work for others to use in their research. Tracey has difficulty with multi-step logic and reasoning that are required in normal living here on the earth, but she does just fine with the support and help of a loving family.

As a family, we all appreciate Tracey's ready smile and love for all of us. All her siblings make an effort to participate in activities with her—things she can really do herself. We have all learned more about ourselves as we live and work with Tracey. She is an inspiration to all who know her. We love her.

Janet Brough

Beautiful Angels

A Child's Eyes

Childrens' eyes are deep and pure
They radiate love that's enough for all!
But sadly some children's eyes are filled with pain
From a life they didn't choose to obtain.
Some children's eyes have seen too much
Their heavy hearts are closed from being crushed.

When will the sparkle in their eyes return?
No one knows without tender loving care.
The empty blank stare inside those eyes
Is it just a curtain to hide the hurt?
Inside lies a tender heart,
Just waiting for the gift only we can impart.

Just reach out your arms in loving care
A gentle touch can, and will, do much to ease the hurt.
Love: that's all it takes
This perfect medicine knows no mistakes
It seems so simple, but not to all
As children are not one size fits all.
When will your love begin to bloom?
To change the heart that has been bruised

> It really doesn't take too much
> So go quickly and prepare their room.
> Doom and gloom—let's change this tune
> Give these children a chance, to blossom and bloom.
>
> Deana Coreen Kastello

We began our journey three and a half years ago when our thirteen-year-old daughter started bugging us to do foster care. A couple at our church had a four-year-old foster daughter that we had all fallen in love with and since our daughter is an only child, she thought we had more than enough room to have a foster child of our own.

My husband and I discussed this at length and had several conversations with our daughter about the commitment of foster care. Our biggest concern as a family was the fact that we would inevitably become very attached to the child and one day he would have to leave us.

My husband and I are in our forties and were not looking to adopt any children at this time. We did, however agree that if a child came into our home and did not have a good permanent home to go to after being in our care that adoption was not out of the question. It was decided . . . we would do foster care for a couple of years while our daughter was in high school. It would be a fun and challenging adventure!

We began the lengthy licensing process and eagerly awaited the day we would become licensed foster parents. We attended classes, had our home inspection, and finally my daughter and I went to the mail one day and our license had arrived! We literally ran back to our home to share the news with my husband.

Then we waited. We had our license, we knew there was a tremendous need for good foster parents, but where were the kids? We were ready—room painted, beds adorned with "Dora the Explorer," and arms ready for hugs. A couple of more days went by and we were getting very disappointed. I phoned our Christian Family Care worker and she explained that it isn't easy as kids in need and foster homes with waiting beds, it needs to be a good fit so that the kids remain in your home and do not get disrupted. I didn't like that answer and didn't understand it at the time.

Here we had waited all of this time for our license and we still couldn't get kids?

I was persistent, so she called one day and said there was a Lodestar meeting being held that evening which would show videos of children. Foster parents could attend and be matched with the children. My husband had school that evening, but my daughter and I jumped in the car and drove downtown, certain that we were going to know that night who our new foster child would be. We had been licensed for young children in the newborn to six-year-old category. We sat and watched the video getting more disappointed all the while as each child they showed was beyond the age we were licensed for. We had no idea however that God had a plan in the works and it would indeed start that evening at that Lodestar meeting. After the video was shown, I was introduced to Charlie Holt of Child Protective Services. He assured me he would look at his list when he got to the office the following morning and see if he had any children fitting our age range. We were willing to do a sibling group of two.

He phoned the next morning and said he did have two little Hispanic girls ages two and three, but they were already doing visits with another family who spoke some Spanish. We do not speak any Spanish. He would keep looking and let me know. By now I was being very persistent and actually went to our agency to search the list myself. Of course I did not know at the time that God had a plan unfolding and well, sometimes I am not very patient with these things! Over the next few weeks there were a couple of sibling groups that we almost got, and then things would fall through at the last minute. I could not understand what was happening. There was such a need, yet we still had no children in our home. Then we got the call. It was Charlie Holt, telling me that the two little Hispanic girls who had been doing visits with another family might be available. He was hesitant to place them with us, however, because they were Spanish-speaking only and well, we were not. We said we would do a visit with them and just see if we could communicate.

My husband, daughter, and I met at the shelter on a Tuesday afternoon. One beautiful little girl with dark skin, a little bob haircut, and the longest eyelashes we had ever seen stood in the living room staring out the window. A few minutes later we were told that she was the three-year-old. Shortly after, another little girl was brought into the living room. She looked tiny for her two years, walked with a limp, and had almost no hair. We filled out the necessary paperwork, and then it was time to begin the visit. I think we were as nervous as they must have been. I remember looking into their terrified eyes. While we couldn't have been more excited, to them we were just more strangers and confusion. We took them to the mall and quickly realized that it is not difficult to communicate with a two- and three-year-old even if you speak different languages. The normal course of events is that you visit a few times, maybe even have them stay the night, but we decided right then and there—these were the ones. We did have them one more time prior to picking them up for good, but our first visit was on a Tuesday and they were living with us by Friday of the same week!

Well, I am happy to say that this was two and a half years ago and I have one of them right now waiting for me to finish this story so that I can play barbies! You see, we did not know the night we went to that Lodestar meeting that the two little girls we would eventually have in our home would be our daughters, but God did. It has not always been easy, and for many months it was an emotional roller coaster after we fell in love with them and then didn't know if they would be returning to their biological mother. It has been the journey of a lifetime, and we have never looked back. It has been one of the most challenging and rewarding things we have ever done.

Our biological daughter is now sixteen and the sisters we are adopting are four-and-a-half and six. One has just finished her first year of school with flying colors and is a happy, well-adjusted young lady who loves books, is a budding artist, and has a great sense of humor. Her tiny little sister has completely caught up in size with other four-year-olds and, instead of walking with a limp, is running so fast we think she may someday run track! Their adoption will be final on June 7 of this year and our family will be complete!

Robert Stiner

Sasha

One day Sasha was lying on my lap.

Sasha rubbed my belly and said, "I was in your tummy."

I said, "Oh honey, you were in my heart. Wyatt was in my tummy, but you were in my heart, where all the love is! A wonderful woman in Korea had you for us."

Sasha said, "I know I was born in Korea, but I was in your tummy!"

Just then something dawned on me. I had had four miscarriages before I conceived Sasha's brother Wyatt. Each time I was so sure I was going to have a girl that when at the end of my pregnancy with Wyatt we were told, "It's a boy!" I was so surprised.

So I said to Sasha, "So you were in my tummy, but you were born in Korea by a wonderful woman?"

She looked me at me with such conviction, "Yes!" Then she smiled and lay her head back on my stomach.

As soon as Wyatt could talk, he kept asking for his sister. We continued to try to conceive, so we kept telling him that you can't choose whether you have a boy or a girl. But he just wanted his sister.

Finally after never getting pregnant, we told him that we had an idea that could make sure he had a sister. We could adopt.

Wyatt was so thrilled. He couldn't wait.

But wait he had to with the long adoption process. One night after a year or so I found him crying in his bed. He was now about 3. I asked him what was the matter. He said, "I am never going to get my sister. It's just always going to be more paperwork!"

It was a difficult process. We had decided to go through the foster care system to adopt. Unfortunately the policy at the time was "return to parent." There were absolutely no children available. Caucasian children that is. They wouldn't let us have an African American baby. The social worker said that we were "too white" and "the child would not be able to relate to you."

All the while, Wyatt was gravitating to every Asian child that crossed his path. That made us think, why not look into an Asian baby. We asked all our Asian friends for advice and got everyone's blessing. So we went to a Korean adoption orientation. It sounded wonderful, but unfortunately the costs were $18,000 which we did not have. We just had to continue to wait for our baby to find us.

That summer we were in Long Island, NY when 9/11 happened. I quickly met my dear friend near New York City before returning to the town where Wyatt and my husband, Paul, were, so we could then drive back to Arizona the moment the bridges reopened. At my friend's house, she asked me if I could go upstairs and say hello to her elderly husband. I was in such a hurry to get to my family, but I did it anyway. I ran upstairs and said, "Kurt, I am so sorry I can't stay and chat, but I have to get back to Paul and Wyatt." He said rather gruffly, "You have such a wonderful child, why don't you have another?" I told him politely that we had been trying. "Why don't you adopt?" he said abruptly. I explained that we were trying that, too. "What about Korea?" went the contined inquistion. I explained about the money. Astonished he said, "What? I have been working for forty years with the First Lady of Korea donating medical supplies for the orphans of her country. She's always asked how she can repay me."

With that he made a phone call simply barking, "Get my friends a baby!"

I thanked him and left, not sure what had just transpired.

But two days later, en route back to Phoenix, my cell phone rang. The message was from Kurt, "You got yourselves a baby."

Eleven months later Sasha arrived with gifts, photos, and newspaper articles from the First Lady. She was known as the First Lady's baby and they had a big ceremony when it was time for her to depart on her trip. (The airline ticket was the only thing we had to pay for.) We had been invited to attend, but they requested that we not bring Wyatt as they felt at age five he might not handle it well. We were a family and it was Wyatt who never let us give up on his sister, so we graciously declined the invitation, telling them we couldn't leave Wyatt behind.

Sasha was five months old and the happiest baby I had ever seen. She settled right in after her long journey of searching for a way to be born that was a lot more certain than my malfunctioning womb. I imagined her saying to Wyatt after the fourth miscarriage, "I've had enough of this, it's your turn. I'm going on an adventure. Just look for the Asian girl!" That's so like Sasha.

A few years later, Wyatt was listening to the news with me as they reported that a certain bill was adopted. He asked, "How can a bill be adopted? I thought 'adopted' meant to love someone so much, you can't live without them." I told him that I guessed that they loved that law that much!

On one particularly exhausting day, free-spirited Sasha had wiped me out, but now was angelically napping. I looked at our beautiful girl and remarked to Wyatt how glad I was that I had never gotten pregnant again. Wyatt said, "Why, because she would have kicked you so hard!"

I knew he was absolutely right. Sasha was always Sasha—our daughter who was going to find us one way or another. The same little soul that had tried so hard to make it work in my tummy was incredibly resourceful and determined. I said, "Exactly, Wyatt!"

Diana Davis

If we ever see the lady in Korea who had me for us, we should really thank her.

—Sasha

His Sweet Little Face

I didn't come out of my mother.
I don't have my father's green eyes.
No one in my family looks like me.
People are always surprised.

I think we're a happier family
Than if we were all kings and queens.
We're so lucky we all found each other.
That's what being adopted means.

Pamela Espeland and Marilyn Waniek

When I was married only about two weeks and was not yet aware of the future struggles that I would have with infertility, I had a vivid and memorable dream. In my dream, I was in the backyard and it was a warm sunny day. I was playing back there with a little boy who was about two years old. He had a happy little face with golden hair and blue eyes. I felt an incredible amount of love for this little boy. He didn't speak; he just stayed near me, looking at me and smiling. I felt that he belonged to me, but I was not sure. I asked him if he was *my* little boy. He nodded yes and smiled. I could sense that he was there to assure me that he was mine. I asked him again if he was sure. He again nodded to affirm that he was my little boy. I was surprised because he was so fair and both my husband and I have dark hair and eyes. I felt closeness to this precious little boy in my dream and I just watched him and studied him. I memorized his little face, and when I woke up I could still see it in my mind and I could still feel his presence. The feelings were so strong that I wanted to share it with my husband. I woke him up and told him of the dream I had just had and I told him, "I don't know how or when, but if my dream comes true, one day we will have an adorable little boy with blond hair and blue eyes. If I could put his face onto a picture from my mind, I could show you what he'll look like." I always remembered that dream and was so glad when we welcomed our third child to our family: a little boy with blond hair, blue eyes, and a bright cheery smile.

The birth mother of our third child lived with us during her pregnancy. In many ways it was a good experience as I was able to closely follow along through the pregnancy with her and feel like I was a part of things. In other ways it was hard because I was constantly worried and wondering if she was going to change her mind, and I didn't know how I would deal with that disappointment and heartache. On one particular night, we were laying on my bed watching TV. It happened to be a movie about adoption. During the movie, the birth mother kept saying to me, "Feel my stomach, he is kicking and kicking!" Each time I would feel . . . nothing! No movement at all. In fact throughout the pregnancy I had never once been able to feel the movements that she so often talked about. I began to feel insecure and sad about not being able to be the one who felt him move. I had a hard time even thinking of this child, whom someone else was carrying inside of her body, as *mine*. Again the birth mother asked me to feel her stomach. "He is really active tonight," she said. I really didn't want to but also did not want to hurt her feelings so I let her take my hand and place it on her stomach. As I did, I said out loud to the baby, "If you know who I am and if you are my baby then please let me know." Suddenly I felt the most definite, strong, real movement. It was so powerful that it left no doubt in my mind that he was sending me a clear message. Both the birth mother and I cried and were touched by the knowledge that we were sharing a very special experience that bonded us in a unique way.

Jona Webb

My Michael

Not flesh of my flesh
Nor bone of my bone
But still miraculously my own.
Never forget for a single minute
You didn't grow under my heart
But in it.

My journey with adoption began as a single, white woman in her early thirties. I was already in the field of child social services (working for a private agency, not a state agency) so I was somewhat familiar with the process of adoption. Through my work travels, I had met a boy named Michael and I was informed that the state was terminating the parental rights.

The current foster family was an older couple not interested in adoption and I was told that Michael would be placed for adoption by an unknown family. They would begin the process of looking for a family when parental rights were terminated, which probably would not occur for at least another year. Michael would remain in foster care until rights were terminated and an adoptive family was located. Michael was already three years old so potentially he would not be with his permanent placement for, at the very least, a year and a half.

When I met Michael, we connected right away. He was sweet, caring, good-natured, and funny but also sad. He had a history of neglect and at the age of three was already in his fourth foster placement. For many weeks, I was extremely distraught about Michael moving to an unknown family. Unfortunately race plays a role in adoption as well. I knew that the odds weren't good for an African-American child with mild special needs being placed for adoption around four to five years of age. This is considered school age, and with every year it becomes more difficult to find a family.

My soul was tortured, thinking who will this family be? Will they treat him well? Will they love him? Respect him? Advocate for him? Would they allow him to keep in touch with his birth family? And will they enforce the importance of college?

I started thinking, should I consider adoption? I was in a different place than most people considering adoption. It found me; I was not seeking adoption. Michael was a state child and if I was interested, I would have to start the process (training and paperwork). My thoughts kept racing back and forth. *I can't do this emotionally or financially.* Then I would go back to, *Yes, I am a strong woman and love children and I love Michael.* I knew I connected to him and I knew he connected to me. The love was there, but it was daunting to be a single white woman adopting an African-American boy. By the way, at the time the race issue was at the bottom of the list. I knew it would have some impact but I was committed to keeping him connected to his birth siblings and for some reason I knew I could make it work. I knew I desperately wanted children, although I imagined it through a committed relationship. It was something I always wanted in life, and I wasn't willing to sacrifice it so I decided to take the plunge. After the initial shock from my immediate family, they were nothing but supportive. They embraced Michael, and race was never an issue.

I did meet a wonderful man and married when Michael was seven years old. I went on to have two biological children. What's funny is that I thought being a single mother to one child would be so difficult but once we got into our routine it was great. I did not experience true stress until I became a wife and added two more children. Michael and I always joke about how at one time it was just us, and he reminds the younger ones that "it was just Mommy and me a long time ago." I have kept Michael connected to a few of his biological siblings. (He is one of seven—with three siblings being adults.) He also has an open invitation to connect with his birth mother at any time. To date, he has not asked for this opportunity. However, since the day he arrived he has had photos of his birth mother and siblings all around his room. I never see him specifically looking at the pictures but I guess he knows they are there. I imagine there is some comfort just knowing he has that opportunity if or when he wants to connect. It is important for adoptive children to know who they look like (if possible) and to feel connected to some birth relation. No matter what your feelings are about a birth mother, it is important to maintain positive feelings about the birth family and have positive thoughts. No matter how well your adoptive child acclimates to your environment, you must always maintain a balance. In simplistic terms, I let Michael know that his birth mother loves him but was unable to care for him. As he has gotten older, he's realized you have to work to have a house over your head; and a car; and to pay for groceries, clothes, and recreation. Now in my case, I know Michael's birth mother loved him. Maybe others will not know this, but as an adoptive mother you have to believe that the birth mother had some warm feelings for this child and would want the best for him. It is important to convey this as you do not want your child to feel unloved and rejected by his birth parents.

My middle child, who now has an understanding about adoption, made a comment about Michael having more than one mother. I stated to my three children who were all together at the time, how lucky Michael is to have two families that love him. Whenever, I get the opportunity to turn adoption comments into a positive message, I do. There are still many negative connotations out there that repeatedly tell our children that they are different or instill in our children that sense of rejection from their birth parents. They do not need any help in this area as our children will always, at some time in their life, wonder why their birth parents didn't keep them and want to know if somehow they had something to do with that decision.

When I read celebrity magazines or other media outlets, I get so outraged when they refer to a child as an adopted child. Why? Why do we keep telling our children they are adopted? Does the media think the adoptive parent or child forgot this? The parent has a child; how the child got here is irrelevant. Will the media soon let us know when showing a picture of a celebrity and her child that the child was a product of infertility treatments? News flash: here is so-and-so's child who was conceived through in vitro fertilization. How ridiculous!

I remember taking Michael to see a kids' movie when he was around six years old. It was a big hit movie in the theatres, and I was shocked and amazed because there was a negative comment about adoption in this animated movie. I attempted to contact the movie company but was unsuccessful. I did contact a well-known adoption advocacy group to inform them about this particular movie. As adoptive parents, we need to continuously make this world a better place for our children. Always advocate for change when change is due—whether it is in your school system, within your extended family, or within the greater systems.

Michael is now twelve years old. Sibling contact does take effort as you are working with other families to arrange get-togethers but Michael has been lucky that his siblings' adoptive parents have the same goal that I do, which is to keep the children connected. Unfortunately, two of his siblings moved out of state last year, but we are still keeping the contact going through emails, phone calls, and pictures. We are hopeful for some visits when the opportunity presents itself.

I tell Michael all the time that my hope for him is that when he is an adult he will have his birth brother and sisters and his brothers that he grew up with all sitting at his Thanksgiving table. At this age, he can't really fully understand my vision. This is my wish because I have always enjoyed Thanksgiving. There is no distraction of gifts; it's purely a day to be thankful and enjoy your family. I hope I am around to see all my children and Michael's siblings (whom I love as well) enjoying this day. I will really feel a sense of accomplishment when this happens and I wait with bated breath to experience this joyous day.

I believe at different times developmentally, children will have questions and thoughts regarding adoption. At this stage, at least for Michael, it is not an area he wants to get into at any length. I will push a little for communication, then respect his wishes, reminding him that the door is always open for conversation. Michael is aware that I speak with his birth mother sometimes and that I know how to get in touch with her. At some point, I imagine he will want to have contact. Right now, he is really into his friends and hardly wants to talk to me. I do not think he wants two mothers in his life right now. I am curious, though, how it will play out in the future.

Birth parents can be a threat; it's a very vulnerable situation to be in when your child has contact with a birth parent. I think that's part of the adoption journey for a child and the adoptive parents. I believe a child has to have some element of control. Of course, every situation is different, every child has a different history, every birth parent and adoptive parent has a different history. This is just my story and my beliefs as I am lucky enough to remain in the field of adoption. As my child has grown, I have become that much more knowledgeable through work with my clients and the trainings I attend, not to mention what my own son has taught me.

Michael is twelve years old now and is doing well. He is involved in track and football. He has many friends and is a very social person. We live in a town that is predominately white, but there are other children who are African American, Hispanic, Asian, and a mix of other cultures. Michael is extremely happy with our community. As with any parent, I hope I am instilling good values, teaching acceptance and tolerance, and emphasizing the importance of education and the importance of family. As I tell Michael, he just came to me differently than his brothers. He was born in my heart and not in my tummy. A long time ago.

His Mother

Abounding Joy

For I was hungry and you gave me something to eat, I was thirsty and you gave me something to drink, I was a stranger and you invited me in, . . .
The King will reply, "I tell you the truth, whatever you did for one of the least of these brothers of mine, you did for me."
Matthew 25:35,40

There was a period of time in my life when I thought I might never be a mother.

Like so many foster and adoptive parents, my husband and I happened upon this journey through the agonizing forests of infertility. I am not one to sit around and wish things would happen, so my husband and I decided to proactively seek parenthood.

A series of events found us in a position to be able to open our home to foster children in the summer of 2000. We hoped that we might be able to foster a young child and maybe eventually adopt, if that became the plan for that child. We were fortunate that the training and approval process moved very swiftly for us. We initially inquired about foster care in February 2000, were approved by June 2000 as a foster and adoptive home, and received our first placement in July 2000. We fostered a thirteen-year-old young man temporarily for a month and helped him move into a more permanent placement. From him we learned that opening our home meant sometimes moving out of our comfort zone, but the blessings come from helping any child are worth the time and effort spent.

We did not have much time to contemplate all that we had learned in that short month, however, because early in August we welcomed our two oldest children into our home. These children, a precious six-year-old little girl and an active, loving little four-year-old boy, brought with them two short lifetimes of hurt and challenges.

We quickly learned that the role of foster parent is not one for the weak or faint of heart. Many behavioral challenges—the effects of abuse and multiple moves in foster care—proved to be challenges that these children would carry with them to some degree throughout their lives. We sought help from every source that we could find. We counseled with therapists, worked with our children's caseworkers, sought information about these children's backgrounds from CASA workers and former foster parents, and read a great deal of information about a number of topics. The time came for the parental rights to be terminated for these two children, and we made the decision to be the last stop for these kids in their journey. All four of us committed to work together to build a family.

As our little family was developing, and as we were ironing out the kinks that had presented themselves, my husband received a phone call from the social services office that they had a sibling group of three that were in need of a home. These children were three very young children: a little blonde haired boy that was five, a precious curly haired girl who was three, and a baby of fifteen months with blue eyes and a smile that would melt the hardest of hearts. We were told from the beginning that it was likely that these children would eventually become available for adoption, and we felt that we would be able to complete the large family that we now wanted all at once. As predicted these children soon became available for adoption, and we felt there could be no greater joy.

We were mistaken. Greater joy came in the arrival of not one but three bouncing baby boys in three years. The biological mother of our sibling group of three gave birth to three new additions to our family.

Our family seemed complete. Imagine our surprise when two years after our youngest son was placed with us, a beautiful baby girl arrived that was a part of the same sibling group.

The limit for the number of children that are placed in a foster home is five, with the only exception being in the case of biological siblings. We joyfully welcomed each baby and, as stated above, have adopted the first three. We have learned of the importance to children and to adoptive families of maintaining sibling bonds whenever humanly possible. These children need each other and evidence of the importance of keeping them together continues to surface daily. We continue to foster our youngest daughter and to work with the biological parents in their efforts to strengthen themselves and become able to care for this child. We will gladly welcome her into our forever family through adoption if that is what is determined to be best for her.

The challenges of rearing a large family are strongly outweighed by the blessings that come from making a forever commitment. Many of the challenges are easily conquered—buying a fifteen passenger van, purchasing a larger home and moving to the country, and learning to cook for "an army." Some of the challenges require perseverance and are ongoing endeavors—learning to live with mental health disorders, overcoming the challenges of developmental delays, and helping the older children to work through the hard things through which they have lived. One thing is for sure . . . there is abounding joy in this journey!

Willa

$200 in Pregnancy Tests!

Trust in the Lord with all thine heart;
And lean not unto thine own understanding.
In all thy ways acknowledge him, and he shall direct thy paths.
Proverbs 3:5-6

Our story of adoption started about seven years ago, when our oldest son was five years old and our second son was three. We were able to get pregnant so easily with our first two, that I arrogantly thought I wanted to wait before having any more children. So we waited until I thought I had a handle on the two we already had.

Because it'd been so easy with our sons, we carefully planned the month to get pregnant, so that I would have the baby in the month I wanted. We also read a book on how to have a girl, since I only wanted to get pregnant with a girl. I was so selfish. When I didn't get pregnant within the first couple of months that we started trying, I was a little disappointed. Little did I know that it was the beginning of five years of disappointment.

After our second son was born I had started having problems with my menstrual cycles. I started having my periods twice a month instead of once and they were very painful. I also seemed to bleed a lot more than normal. So I went to my ob/gyn and he decided I needed to go on birth control pills to regulate my cycles, which was fine with me because, like I said, I didn't want any more kids until our second was a little older. Well, the pills helped and everything was fine until I went off the pills so we could start trying for our third child. All the symptoms came back but they weren't consistent. Honestly, I just thought I was one those people who had really bad, painful periods, but nothing more than that.

So, we kept trying. I kept a perfectly charted calendar. I kept track of my monthly cycles like it was life and death. And each month around the time I was supposed to start my period, I'd hurry over to Wal-Mart and get one those early pregnancy tests. It'd always say "not pregnant," and I'd get so frustrated. I mean, didn't my Heavenly Father know that this was the time I had designated to get pregnant? This went on for about six months and about two hundred dollars' worth of pregnancy tests. Also, I just realized that I probably should have prefaced this whole story with the fact that before all this happened, I was the *least* patient person I had ever known. So, six months seemed like six years to me, my whole life was consumed with getting pregnant. I shared my stress and frustration with my husband (the *most* patient person I've ever known) and he'd try to comfort me by saying "everything is fine" and "we will get pregnant soon." This phrase worked for the first six months and then it just started annoying me. He also told me I should stop stressing about it and stop buying pregnancy tests like they were going out of style. So I did what any impatient woman would do, I stressed more and started hiding the pregnancy tests from him. I also started praying like I had never prayed before—and my prayer was always the same, please help me get pregnant this month, please, please, please! So six months turned into a year and then two years, and still no pregnancy.

At this point I had moved past the denial stage and was in the angry, bitter phase. It seemed like everywhere I looked there was a pregnant person, and I hated them. My friends tried to be helpful, but unless you've gone through it, you really don't know what it feels like. They would say stuff like "well, at least you already have two kids," this came from my friend who was pregnant with number four. I always pretended like I didn't really care and that it didn't bother me when someone I knew got pregnant, but secretly I fumed with jealousy and rage. I started thinking God didn't care about me after all. I kept praying though, just in case, and the answer to my prayers was always the same, "be patient." The thought came unbidden after all my prayers. *Be patient?* Didn't He know I was the least patient person alive? Was He trying to teach me a lesson? If this was so, I wasn't yet ready to deal with it. I was too wrapped up in what I wanted.

Another year went by. During this year I realized something was wrong. Actually I started hoping there was something wrong; something broken that could be fixed easily. I kept telling my patient husband that something was wrong with my body or his body. He didn't believe me. He would say, "You're just stressing too much," and "If you'd stop thinking about it you would probably get pregnant," or his other favorite phrase: "God will send us a baby when it's the right time." I love my husband, and he is wonderful and caring, but he just didn't get it. So I made an appointment with my ob/gyn against my husband's wishes. I had to know; I was obsessed with knowing if something was wrong—if there was a reason why I couldn't get pregnant. Off to the doctor I went. I told him about my irregular menstrual cycles and the fact that we'd been trying to get pregnant for three years. He thought I might have endometriosis.

My younger sister had endometriosis, but hers was so bad that she'd been bedridden for a week every month and eventually had to have a hysterectomy in her twenties. That didn't sound like what I had, but he said he'd need to do a laparoscopy surgery to see for sure what was going on inside me. Since that was the only procedure covered by our insurance, I told him to sign me up. Well, the surgery confirmed it, I had had endometriosis for years and never known it, and it had been so bad that it had permanently scarred my fallopian tubes, making it impossible for me to get pregnant. I was sad, but also relieved to know there was actually a reason why we weren't getting pregnant

After the surgery we spent a few months discussing options—adoption was not one of them. We would go to a fertility specialist and see what could be done. Right away, I didn't like our fertility doctor; although he was supposed to be wonderful. The waiting room was always filled with other angry, bitter, disillusioned women. And it was going to cost a fortune. But, we wanted another child, so we kept going. The doctor told me I was "old" in fertility years, I had just turned thirty. He also told us he'd try drugs first, but most likely I would only get pregnant by in vitro fertilization, which would cost $25,000–$30,000. It didn't matter; my husband and I were on a mission. We were ready to sign our lives away to get pregnant. Before they could start the drugs or the in vitro I would have to one small test done first—an HSG test—that's where they shoot dye into your uterus to clear the fallopian tubes. I told them it wasn't necessary because my ob/gyn had just done that procedure to me while he was performing my other surgery and we were told that my tubes were permanently blocked, but the fertility doc insisted, so I went to get my HSG test. Right before we left for the doctor's office to get the test done, I had my husband say a special prayer for me to calm my nerves. That prayer ended up being the answer I had been seeking for so long. While he was a praying I felt a calm, peaceful feeling wash over me, and for the first time in four years, I knew God was watching over us and that everything was going to be okay.

The test didn't go as planned, it showed my fallopian tubes to be totally open and unblocked—the exact opposite of what our ob/gyn had said. We thought it was a miracle and now we would finally get pregnant. We went home and tried for a couple more months, but nothing happened. We knew for sure though that the drugs and in vitro route was not the path we were supposed to be on. I started praying again, but my prayers changed, I had finally come to that point that we all have to get to in this life. I completely surrendered. Instead of praying that I would get what I wanted, I prayed that I would be able to accept whatever He had planned for me. I no longer felt bitter or angry. I had peace. I had hope. I knew He loved me and everything would work out for our benefit. It was around this time that my husband and I finally broached the subject of adoption. It still wasn't our first choice, but we said, "Let's get certified just in case." We were still thinking I'd get pregnant, but adoption would be our back-up plan.

We called the adoption agency that's run by our church and set up our first appointment. We went away feeling a little overwhelmed, but determined to explore other avenues of bringing a child to our home. We had no idea of the miracles that were about to touch our lives.

The agency sent us home with pages and pages of paperwork that would need to be filled out before we could start the certification process. They also told us that it usually took two years for a baby to be placed with a family once they were certified. It's amazing what you have to go through to be a parent by adoption. They wanted to know every thought we had ever had, every action we had ever taken, and everything about our siblings and parents. I started on the paperwork right away; it felt good to have something to do—some way of moving forward on a path. I zoomed through all of my history and then started on my siblings. I had talked to all my siblings except one—my younger sister. I hadn't talked to her in about a year. She had left her family and gotten sucked into the drug world. She was unrecognizable from her old self and wanted nothing to do with her family, so you can imagine that I was hesitant to call her. Since we hadn't spoken in so long, she had no idea that I was trying to adopt or even that I had been trying to get pregnant for so long.

I finally got my courage up and dialed her number. She seemed happy to hear from me, and I started to tell her that we weren't able to have children of our own and so we had decided to try and adopt. Before I could finish my sentence, she got really excited and said she was living with a friend who was seven months pregnant and wanted to give her baby up for adoption and did we want it? I was shocked! And a little apprehensive.

I asked a bunch of questions. I wanted to know all about the birth mother. Was she sure she wanted to give the baby up for adoption? Did she do drugs? What was she having? Could we come meet her? I was excited but cautious. I hung up and called my husband. We thought it was a miracle, the answer God had been waiting to send us. But, I needed to meet her to be sure. I was very nervous about her being a drug addict and how that would affect the baby, but I also felt guilty for thinking those things, it wasn't the baby's fault that her birth mother had a drug problem. In the end, we decided this was a gift from God and we needed to pursue it.

We were finally able to meet her, she was living in rather deplorable conditions, but she was kind and loving and just wanted to find her baby a good home. The moment I saw her I knew it was right. After that everything happened so fast. The adoption agency had to put a rush on our certification. We had to raise the money to pay for the adoption real fast; luckily we had wonderful friends and neighbors who threw us a huge community garage sale to help pay for the adoption. We lost contact with the birth mom several times; she was homeless and wandered from friend to friend. Luckily, my sister was able to find her and make sure she knew how to get a hold of us. There were a few times I thought it wasn't going to happen; she seemed so flaky. I still worried about the effects of the drugs on the baby. But all of that took second place to the feeling in our hearts that this was the right course—the course our Heavenly Father wanted us to be on.

The night she finally had our little girl, I couldn't sleep all night. I kept waiting for her to call us and tell us we could come down to the hospital to see her. I kept worrying that she'd change her mind. I literally made myself physically ill with worry. I am so grateful for my sister. Even though she was still heavily entrenched in the drug world and was high constantly; she was still able to be the mediator between the birth mom and us. My sister was able to talk to the birth mom the morning after giving birth to our little girl, Raya. The birth mom told us we could come down and get her as soon as possible. We rushed to the hospital five hours after Raya was born, and the birth mom handed us our baby. It was amazing. I realized this really was going to happen. We were going to be parents again. The hospital was wonderful and gave us our own room down the hall to stay with Raya until she could come home with us.

When the birth mom came in to give birth she was high on drugs, so the hospital had to specially monitor Raya's little body. To everyone's amazement, she was perfectly healthy. We took her home two days later. She has never shown any signs of the effects of the drugs. She has been the joy of our lives. Never was a child wanted or loved more than we love our Raya. My heart was at peace and I finally knew what God was trying to tell me. "Be patient," He whispered to my heart over and over again. For five long years I was forced to be patient, and it was worth every minute of it for what I learned: unconditional love, faith, humility, and how to surrender my will to His will. I wouldn't trade those lessons for all the children in the world. And God wasn't through with his miracles.

In the year following Raya's birth, we lost contact with the birth mom. My sister had been arrested on drug-related charges and was in jail awaiting trial. She had always been our link with the birth mom, but now she also had no contact with the birth mom for about a year. Another six months went by and out of the blue my sister called me from jail to say that the birth mom had also been recently arrested on drug charges and coincidentally put in the same jail dormitory as my sister. The birth mom had also just given birth to a second baby girl. She was overjoyed to see my sister and begged my sister to contact us and see if we would please try to get custody of the baby and try to adopt her. We were in shock. Another baby? What a blessing.

We made some calls and discovered that the little girl was already three months old and had been living in a foster home since birth. We called Child Protective Custody and got a hold of the caseworker in charge of the case. She seemed optimistic about our chances to adopt the baby. Since we already had Raya and they would be related by blood, the laws in our state were on our side. We had to get recertified and there was a small legal battle with the foster parents. They wanted to keep her, which I totally understood, but we were convinced that the baby needed to grow up with her sister and that God wanted her with us. We persevered and when she was six months old, we got custody of our second little girl, Jacy. We have since adopted her. Like her older sister Raya, she is perfectly healthy, with seemingly no side effects from the drug abuse. We are truly blessed. The journey of adoption was the hardest and most wonderful experience of our lives. And because of our experience we have been able to influence other families struggling with infertility to explore the adoption route.

Julie Porter

By the Grace of God

God sets the lonely in families.
Psalm 68:6

    While attending the National Foster Parent Association yearly conference in Minnesota, I received a call from my husband who told me that he had just taken an emergency placement. It was a seven-year-old red-headed, green-eyed little boy needing an immediate foster home and my husband, with his big heart, took him. But, he said, "He'll probably be gone before you get home next weekend." But all foster parents know how that goes. After almost eleven years, he's still here for every day and every weekend.

    When I was picked up at the airport by my husband and this child, I immediately felt he had found a home with us until a permanent could be reached for him, but I never dreamed that his permanent home would be mine.

    I have always felt that, if possible, as visits with birth families occur, foster parents need to establish a good relationship with the birth families. This will go a long way in helping the child, particularly if permanency means going back home. I felt that the weekly visits with Kenneth's mom and dad were very positive, but their parental rights were determined by the department.

    Kenneth was not eager to be adopted by anyone as his mom had told him that he would have to go with what the court decided until he was older, but at eighteen he could come home.

When Kenneth was twelve we were told, "Adopt him or he'll be moved." My husband and I decided that this had been Kenneth's home for five years, and we couldn't see him being moved. I had prayed and felt that this young man needed the opportunity to make a future for himself, and even if he wanted to return home, right now our home was his home.

My husband was diagnosed with terminal lung cancer and was hesitant to adopt—thinking of me raising a boy, going through those dreaded teen years by myself—but that didn't stop the adoption procedures. Kenneth was very opposed to any adoption, and it was through my insistence with the department that I arranged a visit in my home with his birth parents who had had their parental rights terminated. They helped convince Kenneth that the best thing for him would be to stay with us and not to be moved to a strange and new adoptive placement.

To shorten the long story, although too young to be able to make that decision, Kenneth finally agreed, with hesitation, and the adoption was finalized one month before my husband died. I know that it was by the grace of God and prayer that I felt Kenneth was worth saving. He needed the opportunity to continue in my home and to be able to make a successful future for himself.

Today, as we look forward to October when Kenneth will be eighteen years of age, he has requested that his name be changed to mine, which he did not want at his adoption date. He plans to continue in school, and who knows what the future holds? But this I know: I do not resent taking the red-headed, green-eyed, shy, and frightened little boy into our home. He now stands as a son to be proud of.

And what about his birth mom who approved of the adoption? She lives not four miles from us and still has some contact with Kenneth, but she realizes that he is doing well and that they will always be able to have some contact.

I know that God, in his infinite wisdom, sent Kenneth to our home. I know, even with the ups and downs during the past eleven years, it'll be worth it all seeing him grow into a mature, well-adjusted adult.

Betty Hastings

Children will not remember you for the material things you provided, but for the feeling that you cherished them."

—Richard L. Evans

Thank You, Mom!

I was put in foster care when I was seven years old, and the first home I stayed in for about four months. I then got to go back home for about four months, and then back into foster care, which didn't work out and I was moved again. My third placement was in the home of Charles and Betty Hastings. My foster mom was at a foster parent conference and my foster dad was told I would only be there for the weekend, but I stayed for five years, and then my caseworker told me I needed to be adopted.

I didn't want to be adopted at first, but at the age of twelve, my worker, with the help of my foster mom helped me to decide that this was best for me. It was six months before the adoption took place and the judge made special arrangements since my foster dad was very sick with lung cancer.

I had helped my foster dad put up a new ceiling in the dining room and the living room, and we finished right before my adoption. My adoption was May 1, 2003 and my dad died June 1, 2003.

I have an older brother and two older sisters, but I'm the only one still at home.

I am in the ninth grade at school and plan to graduate and go on to college, but I may go into the military first.

I think it is nice for kids that need a family to have parents that can adopt them and give them a good home. I might even consider adopting a child later in my life.

I have my mom and dad to thank for the adoption because if it wasn't for them, I wouldn't be where I am today. I'd probably in a group home or another foster home. I thank them for giving me a good place to come home to.

Kenneth

A Potluck Brought Us Five Little Ducks

And all things, whatsoever ye shall ask in prayer, believing, ye shall receive.
St Matthew 21:22

I was at a mother-daughter potluck for school when I met the mother of one of my students. Sheila Carr told me that she and her husband were new foster parents. This intrigued me enough to ask questions about foster parenting. Knowing that Sheila had grown children ready to graduate from high school, the pressing question I wanted answered was this, "Why would you want to foster parent at this time in your life?" Sheila answered in her sweet, soft-spoken southern accent, "Well, I just wasn't done mother'n yet." Those words pierced my heart. I immediately went home and told my husband, Rande, what Sheila had said. I put Sheila's telephone number in my nightstand—I had a strong premonition that one day I might need Sheila. Rande had a son from his previous marriage. Jane, Rande's ex-wife, and I have a great relationship. The three of us decided it would be in Jack's best interest to have siblings. I always wanted a big family, so we were ready to start building. Rande always joked with me that "eight was enough." I said I would hold him to that.

Our first foster children came ten months after we were married. Steven and his brother were excited to have a mom and a dad. Jack was six, and adjusted fairly well to sharing his toys, bedroom, and his father with two boys. I would cuddle Steven at night as he cried, "My real mom would put me to bed without breakfast, lunch, or supper. When I was cold, she would sit me near a window and rub my cold hands and feet." Steven came into our home with serious coordination issues. For example, at age five he could not alternate his feet going up and down the stairs. He didn't learn how to ride a bike until he was seven and even then, he couldn't understand how to use the brakes. He is now thirteen and his handwriting looks like that of an eight-year-old. He has had extensive vision therapy, but he will always struggle with hand-eye coordination. His disabilities are not obvious, but he struggles with daily activities that most of us take for granted. His brother had serious psychological needs and required institutionalization. We worked with him for nine months, but realized he needed more than we could provide. Steven, at age five, stayed with us. We welcomed Steven's mother into our home and tried to keep open communication between Steven and his birth family, particularly his birth sister, Stephanie, who remained with her birth father. Three years later, parental rights were terminated and we made the decision to adopt Steven, who was then eight years old.

Stephanie was recently brought back into Steven's life when Rande recognized her at a vocal concert in Cedar Rapids more than a year ago. He approached her and asked, "Are you Stephanie and did you have a little brother named Steven?" She smiled and quietly said, "Yes." After a short chat, Rande gave her his telephone number and asked that she first ask permission from her father and then call Steven if she wanted to spend time with him. Before she left the concert, she said, "I remember the last time I saw your family was on Easter Sunday five years ago." She was absolutely right. We had impacted her life more than we had ever realized. Stephanie did call a few days later and asked if she could spend the day swimming with Steven at our home. Rande picked her up at her home and brought her over to spend the day swimming and visiting. Stephanie looked so much like Steven. She was tall and thin. She came over again later in the summer, but then she and her father moved away. Steven does not have a big interest in maintaining a relationship with Stephanie, but at one point in his life he will.

A few weeks after Steven's brother left our home, the department called asking if we would like a three-and-a-half-year-old little girl. We immediately accepted Meranda into our home. Without specific details, let's just say that Meranda needed a very safe environment where the men in her life would treat her as a little girl. Meranda was in play therapy for three years and at the age of ten has finally come to terms with her abuse. She is a gifted artist and constantly engages herself in artistic activities.

Just three weeks after Meranda was brought to us, Meranda's baby sister, Lexi, needed a foster home. Meranda had been removed from her father's care, and Lexi had been removed from her mother's care. Meranda had no idea she even had a baby sister. Lexi was nine months old and living in a temporary foster home. Lexi arrived at our home with a letter from her temporary foster mom, it started out, "Dear Rande and Lora.... I'm so happy to know where Lexi will be living." I squealed to Rande to come read the letter; it was from Sheila Carr, the beautiful lady who had gotten us interested in being foster parents. Her abundant love had come full circle! Lexi was a complete blessing to our home. I put a crib in Meranda's bedroom, so the two girls would finally be real sisters.

Steven was unhappy about sharing his life with two girls. He was furious! Jack, on the other hand, really enjoyed having two little sisters. He absolutely adored Lexi and read to her constantly. We developed a relationship with Lexi and Meranda's mother and with Lexi's father. We invited their mother over for holidays and birthdays, and met her at parks and at the local swimming pool. Lexi's father came to our home too. We believe in reunification as the purpose of foster care. We also know that should reunification occur, we want to be sure we can continue to see our foster children and be assured of their safety.

Parental rights were eventually terminated for the girls and we adopted Meranda first and Lexi several months later. Meanwhile, baby Sadie arrived rather unexpectedly. I had a student named Danielle. Danielle was particularly fond of me because she knew that I had foster children and Danielle wanted to be a social worker. When she discovered her cousin was pregnant and that the Department of Human Services would remove the baby just after birth, Danielle began her mission of placing this unborn child in a home where she knew the baby would be safe. With the help of her parents, she contacted the department and asked that the baby be placed with us. Danielle and her parents knew the mother was unfit to raise a child and they promised to keep the baby's location private.

When the baby was born early, the department was not informed, so mom and baby went on the run. Eventually they were located. When we took this two-month-old baby home, she smelled of smoke, had dirt corroded beneath her fingernails, and weighed just over five pounds. Our family had grown to five children in just two and a half years. When Sadie arrived, none of the children had yet been adopted. We were getting nervous about being so attached and still being unsure of how these situations might end.

Terminations came and adoptions began. Each termination was contested by the birth parents. Even some extended family members appeared and wanted to stop the adoptions. None of this was easy, but all of it was worthwhile.

Just after Steven and Meranda were adopted, we decided our 1,400 sq. ft. home was too small to raise five children, and perhaps more! We didn't have to look too far to find the perfect home for our growing family. It was one mile from our first home and only half a mile from the school where I teach. It was priced far beyond our means, but I continued to stay positive. We negotiated until the price became a possibility with our lender. Our realtor told us that only a growing family would work in this home, because it was far too big for a typical family.

In August 2004, on the same day Lexi was adopted, we moved into our new home. The house sits on one acre in town in a beautiful newer neighborhood.

Jack is an interesting child who dances to his own beat. His latest philosophical question was, "If there is truly divine intervention, then why worry about human rights?" Jack eased into the big-brother role. Not only is he a big help with the younger children, but he also is an excellent role model. Sadie and Lexi enjoy having Jack read bedtime stories.

Steven, who is thirteen, loves music. He's still somewhat challenged with drawing and writing, but he loves to listen to old music. He has learned to love swimming. Steven also plays tennis, soccer, and baseball. Although he recognizes he is not the most valuable player on the team, he still enjoys each sport and is eager to contribute to the success of his team.

Ten-year-old Meranda is an artist. From the time she was five, she has insisted she will be an artist. Meranda is a daydreamer at school and clearly marches to her own beat. She makes beautiful three-dimensional greeting cards. In her spare time, she creates mathematical challenge questions for her teacher.

Lexi, who is seven, would rather live outdoors than indoors. She collects bugs, ants, snakes, flowers, and rocks. She cries during the summer when she must come inside to clean up for dinner. One might think she's a tomboy, but that's far from the truth. She's a "girly girl" all the way. She loves pink, wears dance outfits, and loves to wear dresses.

Sadie, who is five, is a natural gymnast. She is also an avid computer player. She has mastered Dr. Seuss Preschool, Dr. Seuss Kindergarten, Freddi Fish, Clifford Reading, and Strawberry Shortcake games. Her new interest is in telephone numbers. If you give her your telephone number, she'll memorize it and call you every day!

We have taken children from broken homes and hardship situations and built an amazing family of our own. With five children of our own (Jack and his four adopted siblings) and three additional foster children, we have a beautiful but challenging family. Each day is a new and wild adventure.

Lora Lemkuhl

Our Infertility/Adoption Experiences

Legacy of an Adopted Child

Once there were two women who never knew each other
One you do not remember, the other you call Mother
Two different lives shaped to make you one
One became your guiding star, the other became your sun
The first one gave you life, and the second taught you to live it
The first gave you a need for love, the second was there to give it
One gave you a nationality, the other gave you a name
One gave you a talent, the other gave you aim
One gave you emotions, the other calmed your fears
One saw your first sweet smile, the other dried you tears
One made an adoption plan, that was all that she could do
The other prayed for a child, and God led her straight to you.

Now, which of these two women, Are you the product of?
Both, my darling, Both, Just two different types of love.

Unknown

Our Infertility/Adoption Experiences

I think we knew shortly after we were married that it was going to be a struggle to get pregnant. We even went to our doctor early on. His response: "You have to wait until you've been married three years before worrying about it." Being young, we listened. I know better now. Internal instincts can sometimes be more accurate than medical "advice."

Those three years were extremely hard. The only time in my entire life that I have ever intentionally missed church for no good reason was during that time. I just couldn't take going to church on Mother's Day. We would go to a hotel the Saturday night before and "pretend" that we were out of town. It was just too painful to have to listen to talks on mothers. Fast Sundays were also hard when there were baby blessings. How I longed that it was our baby being blessed!

It was also very hard to be around my husband's family. His sister had gotten married just two months after us and immediately got pregnant. I was pretty bitter, after all we had gotten married first so *we* should have the first grandchild. That pregnancy ended up in a miscarriage and I have always felt a little responsible for that. It didn't help that another sister got married just a year after us and both sisters ended up pregnant soon after. However, we tried to be a good aunt and uncle to those two boys.

We tried infertility treatments for a year. After a while, I just couldn't take the lows that came each month when it didn't work. For us, it just wasn't worth it. So we applied for adoption. I tell you, if *every* parent had to go through what adoptive parents go through there would be a lot of childless couples! All that paperwork! We felt at times like our privacy was being invaded. We had to have the doctor fill out a form "proving" our infertility. There were financial forms, the home study, questions about how we were raised, and questions about our thoughts on discipline. I understand that today an adoptive couple even has to take classes. I understand some of the reasoning for all of this, but it does make you feel a little inferior. After all, they don't make biological parents go through all that. I felt like I was second class since I couldn't get pregnant. At the same time, you are able to tell your children that you really, really wanted them or you wouldn't have put up with all that! Not all biological children can say they were wanted that much.

We were told initially that the wait time was between three to five years. In August 1988, we were at a family reunion and it seemed like everyone was asking us if we knew when we would get a baby. Our response was that it hadn't been three years, so it would be awhile. We got *the call* that night at 11 PM. If we hadn't been at the reunion, we could have found out earlier. We were cautioned to not tell anyone until we made sure that this infant was our son. The meeting was set for 10:00 the next morning. We did not sleep a wink that night! In fact, we were at the store buying diapers, formula, bottles, a car seat, and so forth at midnight! That was a neat experience to finally be able to be in the baby aisle! But it didn't compare at all to the experience of picking up our son.

I fell in love with him the moment I saw him laying in the bassinet with his little behind sticking up in the air. He was so cute and cuddly. He was everything we had ever hoped for! The experience of introducing him to our extended family was also a very precious moment. After six years of agony, it was a very emotional, happy time.

One of the perks of adoption is that the joyful experience does not end with the phone call or the placement, the day you go to court for finalization is also a very special moment. In some ways, it is almost anti-climactic. You spend a lot of time waiting and very little time actually in with the judge. But it is all worth it!

Then comes the trip to the temple to be sealed. It was almost better than our wedding day in that I was not quite as nervous and still got the extra special treatment. The ceremony is very short but worth every bit of it. There was just something extra special about having the same sealer perform this ceremony as had performed our marriage ceremony. A lot of the same family members were there as well. Even the witnesses were the same. Just to keep with the sameness theme—we even had a family dinner after the ceremony.

We have gone on to adopt four more children and each one was a special experience. Our third and fifth child ended up being a different race—African American. Our fourth child is bi-racial. Each one has brought unique and special qualities into our family.

I once heard a social worker say that there is a feeling among some people that adoption is a "second" choice since you can't have your own. I have never felt that my children were "second choices." They were each loved by their birth moms who wanted a better life for them. I consider it a special honor that they have trusted us to give them that better life. I also think that in some ways, adoption is even better! Daniel and I have not passed on any of our "bad" genes to our children. They also have *two* dads and moms. They are in no way "second choices."

Kris Patrick

Still Honeymooning!

*I took the road less traveled by,
and that has made all the difference.*

—Robert Frost

Aloha,

My name is Mark. My wife, Jalene, and I live on the garden island of Kaua'i. We moved here from Arizona seven years ago. As our four boys were all grown and on their own, we decided to become foster parents. We had taken a very extensive training course in Arizona, but had never gotten any foster children. When we got to Kaua'i, we took training again and before our license was in the mail, we got a call from our social worker asking if we would be interested in taking in a brother and sister.

Our social worker said she thought they would be a good match for us, but warned that the boy was turning thirteen in a couple of days. We had discussed taking in only younger children until we got the hang of foster parenting. We had raised four boys through the teenage years and the stories we'd heard of teenage foster children worried us a little. We wanted our first foster parenting experience to be a positive one. But we said, "Okay, let's meet them."

Nick and Teresa were great kids. Nick was very quiet, but Teresa was just the most open, fun, and loving child I'd ever met. After a few minutes of checking out our house, Teresa was snuggled up on the couch next to me, carrying on a great conversation. Nick talked when spoken to, but was very reserved. He did say that he thought it would be good to live with us. He was so quiet; it was hard to believe he was Teresa's brother. But he definitely is. Because of the neglect they had lived in for years, they were the only ones each other could rely on.

We called our social worker the next morning and told her it was a yes. From the time they moved in, we just clicked. It was like love at first sight. Our personalities complemented each others'. Teresa was the peanut butter to my jelly and Nick was the salt to Jalene's pepper.

Jalene and I were amazed at how neglected they'd been. They didn't know basic things like bathing, toilet use, and how to use eating utensils. I remember Nick being amazed at our silverware drawer. He said he'd never seen different sized spoons. The only ones he'd ever seen were teaspoons.

The kids wore the same dirty, wrinkled, unfitting clothes to school every day and both were very small for their ages. We found out from their teachers that they missed a lot of school and always came hungry.

After a couple of weeks, their teachers reported an amazing transformation. They said the kids were quickly developing as better students and having more fun at recess. By the end of the first month, the kids' social worker told us that we were the best match he had ever seen. Not long after that, he said that, though they were doing everything possible to make reuniting with their mother possible, he didn't think it would happen and asked if we would consider adopting them.

From our training and talking to other foster parents, we knew about the infamous "honeymoon period" and my wife worried that things might change as the kids were with us longer. I conceded that it was a possibility, but I felt that what people were saying and what we felt (that this was an extraordinary match) was true.

After Jalene decided that we could find out more about possible adoption, we asked the kids how they felt. Nick, in his understated way said it would be "okay." Teresa about jumped out of her skin with joy. She wanted nothing else.

Still, Jalene was concerned about practical things like: could we afford to raise two kids to adulthood. Fostering is temporary, but adoption is forever and she wanted to be sure that we could take care of them financially. Our social worker said that some financial support was available when adopting.

As time went on, it was obvious that there was no "honeymoon period." This was a perfect match (and it still is). The process of giving the birth mother every chance before severing her rights took two years. By that time, we were a complete family and we all looked forward to the adoption.

And we all lived happily ever after . . . well, not quite yet.

An aunt from the east coast contacted the kid's social worker and said that she wanted to adopt them. The social worker told us that it is state policy to place with blood relatives when possible, so we wouldn't be able to adopt them after all. We were all in shock. We were a wonderful family and had been looking forward to making it permanent for almost two years.

To make a long story short, we felt that it would hurt the children to be ripped from another home and be sent to a really foreign environment. Only if you have lived on Kaua'i can you understand the difference in life on Kaua'i and life on the East Coast of the mainland.

The children's psychologist (who was a very strong proponent of placing with blood relatives) agreed that after two years, the bonding was so strong that it would be detrimental to their well-being to be removed from our home. So we had to go to court and let the judge decide their future.

This was a very tough time for us. Jalene and I had to come to terms with the fact that we could lose these children whom we loved so much—who from the beginning had seemed as much ours as our birth children. Nick's and Teresa's futures, which had been bright and secure, were now unsure. They didn't know where they'd be living in a few weeks. It was all up to the judge.

Well, after a very tense session in court, the judge made his decision in our favor. Jalene cried, and I finally breathed. The kids were in another room. When we told them the judge's decision, Nick quietly approved and Teresa jumped for joy. She asked if she could thank the judge. She went in and gave him a hug and a kiss.

Nick is now eighteen and a freshman at the University of Hawaii on the island of Oahu. This shy kid has come out of his shell thanks in part to joining the high school football team and becoming a star receiver and thanks also in part to becoming the "McDonald's kid." Nick won a contest and had his picture and name on the McDonald's bags and cups around the world for a year and a half. Flying to London with Jalene for

VIP treatment as they took pictures of him and he signed autographs and did interviews brought Nick even further out of his shell. When he finishes college, he wants to be a videographer for NFL films or ESPN.

Teresa is now thirteen and wants to do everything. She has been a cheerleader, played soccer and volleyball. She is an altar server at our church. She has been a junior counselor at the humane society's kid camp. She is the "little mother" of all the younger kids in the neighborhood. When she grows up, she wants to be a pastry chef, a teacher, and lots of other things. Her biggest love is hula. She has danced in shows and competitions for the last six years. In the last few months, she has decided to learn to play ukulele and is now performing with her uke in public.

Jalene and I are so grateful for these two kids. And the most wonderful thing is that they are grateful for us. That is perhaps the greatest gift of adoption. We chose to adopt these two and they chose to be adopted by us . . . and so we appreciate each other that much more.

Mark Huff

Mallory

Children are the bridge to heaven

—Persian quote

After our fourth child turned five years old, I assumed that he would be our last and that no more children would be coming our way. We had a daughter and three sons. Our daughter was twelve and she had really wanted a sister. I told her that that probably was not going to happen in this lifetime. She told me that she had been praying for a sister and that she had also been fasting for one each fast Sunday too. She felt strongly that the Lord would answer her prayers and send her a sister. I believe in prayer and fasting, but I also knew that we already had more children than the amount that they allow through the adoption agency and it didn't seem likely that another adoption would just fall into our laps. I tried not to burst her bubble, but I also tried to let her know that I was sure that the Lord heard her prayers, but that it may not be the exact answer that she was hoping for. She felt certain that she would be blessed with a sister, just like she had prayed for. I said that I thought that would be wonderful if it happened and not really knowing what else I should say to her, I just kind of let it go for the time being.

In the meantime, I had called the adoption agency and told them that I was offering our home to any unwed mother who needed a place to stay during her pregnancy. We had an extra bedroom and although I knew we were not able to adopt any more children (except "special needs" babies) we wanted to help out other couples, families, and the agency. They were grateful for the offer and said that they would call on us if they had a need. I just put it to the back of my mind, thinking that nothing would ever come of it, but that I was willing to help out if it did.

One day about a month or so later, I got a call from the agency asking if our family would be willing to take care of a new baby for a few days after it was released from the hospital while they finalized all of the paperwork and prepared the baby for placement with its new family. We were thrilled with the opportunity and gladly agreed to help out. The baby was not yet born, but they would contact us when that happened. When we got the call, I was feeling sick and felt tempted to tell them that I wouldn't be able to help, but when I heard it was a baby girl, I found myself agreeing to take care of her.

As we made the long drive to pick her up, I remember telling myself not to get attached because it was only temporary. We were only supposed to have her in our home for about three to five days. When I saw her, she was beautiful and she looked very similar to our daughter. We enjoyed caring for this precious baby and although we tried not to—we were bonding with her. Our daughter was delighted to have a "sister" even if it was only temporary. She was very attentive to her and was a big help. I dreaded the call that said our time was up and that they would come to pick her up. When the call did come, it was not what we had expected. Instead of saying that they would be coming to get her, they asked if we would be willing to keep her for another few weeks, because they had run into some problems with the placement. I was more than glad to keep her longer, but I did worry because I was really falling for this sweet little baby and it was impossible to meet her needs and give her comfort and care without becoming attached. Our daughter was feeling the same feelings that I was, and I didn't want to see her get hurt when it was time to give the baby up.

She was a good baby—a pure delight. The whole family was falling in love with her. We were enjoying the experience of having her in our home as a part of the family. Well, a few more weeks turned into a few months and by this time, we were *all* completely attached to and in love with this baby girl. Even our extended family had become attached. How could you not? She needed us, and to give her anything less than all of our love was not fair to her. My heart began to ache at the thought of them taking her away. I felt it only fair to warn the agency of my feelings. I told them that I was willing to keep her as long as was needful, but that if she were with us much longer, I felt that they may have to cut my arms off to take her from me. They then told us that they were surprised that I called when I did because they had just been discussing this case and had come to some decisions and were going to call us and let us know of the developments. As it turned out, they were having serious legal problems regarding this particular placement. In fact the legal problems were so complicated that it was making her placement nearly impossible and they anticipated that it would likely be a long process and they were really unsure at this time of what the final outcome would be. So, they had come to the decision that due to the intense legal problems involved in this particular case, they were going to place this baby girl that we loved so dearly in the "special needs" category.

Now this term usually refers to babies/children with medical or physical challenges or disabilities. In this case her legal issues were her challenge. As it turned out, my husband I had qualified earlier and were on the approved list for adopting "special needs" children. We had wanted to keep our options open and had got on the list for that reason. Since we were able to adopt special needs children and we had had our baby girl for all of her life and we had already bonded with her and loved her as our own, we had the opportunity to have her placed with us for a possible adoption! We had to be willing to accept all of the legal challenges involved with that decision and the possible heartache of losing her if things didn't go in our favor.

We were so in love with her at this point that we didn't even have to think about it, we would do whatever was required to have the opportunity to keep her with us *forever*! It was worth the risk. We wanted her with all of our hearts!

We were grateful for this chance. We were also very worried about the possibility of ever having to lose her, but focused on the fact that she was here with us now, and that she loved us and needed us. As it turned out, the legal battle was long and difficult. It went on for years and at many times we feared that we would lose her. We prayed, we hoped, we waited. Often we cried and always we worried. We would win little victories along the way, only to have everything reopened in a higher court. It was a roller coaster.

In fact, one particular time when things were exceptionally stressful and I was heartsick over another setback and worried how I could ever cope with the reality of losing our precious baby girl, I had a dream. In the dream, she and I were on a wild roller coaster. On the roller coaster with us were all of the attorneys that were working on her case. I looked over at her and her little head was whipping around with the roughness of the ride we were on. Neither of us liked it at all. I asked her if she wanted to get off of the roller coaster and she nodded, yes. We calmly stepped off of it, hand in hand and as we turned back to look, the roller coaster was still running wildly with all of the people in charge of the legalities. She and I knew that they must continue with their necessary work, but that she and I could just focus on being safe and being *together*. Mother and child. I felt calmness come over me that things would be fine. That I just needed to be patient. I felt many of the burdensome worries lift off of me and a spirit of peace settled over me.

In time, the adoption that we had longed for and prayed for was at last finalized in our favor! Words cannot express the gratitude, relief and joy that we all felt! Yes, our oldest daughter was right, the Lord did bless her with a sister after all. He had answered her prayers and we were all blessed because of it. To this day, our fifth and youngest child is still a delight to us all. We love her dearly and cannot imagine what our lives would feel like without her. We would be incomplete. She is an important and irreplaceable part of our family. We know that she was meant to be ours and we will never forget the hand of the Lord in making this all happen—a miracle arranged especially for us.

Jona Webb

Busy, Noisy, and Very Happy!

Be strong and of a good courage, fear not, nor be afraid of them;
for the Lord thy God, he it is that doth go with thee; he will
not fail thee, nor forsake thee.
Deuteronomy 31:6

My adoption story starts thirty years ago, when my husband and I began to realize that we couldn't seem to get pregnant. After a few years of no babies, we started on the fertility road, trying all kinds of tests and experts' opinions. In the meantime, we were moving into our thirties. My husband had said, early in our relationship, that he would like to adopt. I agreed with him, but did want to experience carrying and giving birth to a baby also. So, for us, adopting was never a questionable issue. I had always been a mommy type of person and loved babies and kids of all kinds. Nurturing came very naturally to me. After several years of frustrations of not getting pregnant, we turned in our papers to the state adoption office and were told we would get a child in a couple of years, but only over eighteen months of age. After a few years we received the most amazing call from our social worker that they had a two-month-old baby boy for us to consider. Needless to say, we were thrilled! The next day we began a long trip across our state and had our red-headed son in our arms by the next day. For the next year we were so happy. The arrival of this baby also brought both of us into a spiritual awakening of sorts. Suddenly we realized how important life was and we knew we wanted to do the very best for our son. We also had to acknowledge the wonderful blessing this child was from our Father in Heaven. Thus, our adoption and spiritual stories are quite intertwined.

As time went on, we knew we wanted more children and, so, we applied through our church's social services agency. That wait seemed forever (three years) but finally, five days before Christmas, we were blessed with a beautiful, black-haired, six-day-old daughter. By now our son was weeks away from his fifth birthday, and he worked hard to fill his role of the big brother. At this point we made a difficult and important decision for me to quit my career as a registered nurse and stay home full time with our children. I loved my job and enjoyed helping people but I had waited so many years to be a mommy. That was a tough choice but one I have never regretted.

Because we were reaching our mid-thirties, we decided we didn't have time for more three- to five-year waits for more children. A good friend sat down with me and introduced me to the world of independent or open adoptions. Wow! That really opened up our options and thus began our new journey. I made up about 1,500 resumes about us, complete with a few pictures. I circulated these to doctor's offices, pregnancy crisis centers, and a large midwifery convention. The response was phenomenal and we received several calls from a few attorneys, midwives, and birth moms. We were able to refer several situations to friends who wanted to adopt and we were blessed with two baby girls from two different birth mothers in two different states (the girls are two weeks apart). Suddenly our family was busy, noisy, and happy.

We have really enjoyed the open and loving relationships with each of the birth mothers and we were convinced that open adoption offered wonderful options to all involved. When those two little girls were about two and a half years old we received a special phone call from a birth grandmother (she was only in her forties), whose daughter wanted to do an open adoption for her yet-to-be-born son. She came and spent time with us in our home and she bonded with our whole family. The remainder of the pregnancy went quickly as she, her mother, and all of us grew closer and more excited. As this special little boy was born, I was her coach, and her mother and best friend were also present. It was the most amazing, spiritual experience I could imagine. The Lord most definitely has His hand in where each child is to go and it became so evident to me during this experience. (To this day, this birth mom and I are very close and thoroughly enjoy our special "sisterhood.")

As I looked back on each of our children's arrivals into our family I realized that each baby got younger with each progressive adoption. The oldest had been nine weeks, the next was six days, the third was seventy-two hours, the fourth was fifteen minutes old, and then the fifth I was there as he slipped into the world. I would joke that the only way we could continue this progression was if I gave birth, which seemed completely impossible after seventeen years of no pregnancies. (I was now forty.) But that is exactly what happened! One September morning I found myself taking two different pregnancy tests and they both came back positive! I was astounded and immediately went to share this with my husband. Well, the next nine months were such fun, with few discomforts, and such anticipation. On my forty-first birthday, I gave birth to a beautiful, petite baby girl. What a gift! I came home to an eleven-year-old, a six-year-old, two four-year-olds, and a fifteen-month-old. Boy, did I have my arms full and I was one happy, busy mommy. (I also homeschool!)

We thought we probably were done building our family until one day I got a phone call introducing me to another birth mother. She wanted us to adopt the baby she was expecting since she was already the single mother of five other children. We had a great time together over the next several months and one day in March, she delivered a darling little baby boy into my hands. Her other children were present and bathed in the love we all shared for this little boy.

Today, these precious seven children are growing up so quickly (now thirteen to twenty-seven years old). As I reflect on the special adoption journey we embarked on thirty years ago, I feel such gratitude to Heavenly Father and to each birth mother who brought a baby to us. In fact, as time goes on, I have come to deeply appreciate and better understand the birth mothers everywhere who agonize and sacrifice to make a loving, selfless choice for their babies. I have also become a strong advocate for open adoption as I have observed each of my children mature, feeling loved and secure, and with no secrets or unknown birth mothers. Compassionate adoptions are best for all. Our birth mothers have also matured, healed, and moved forward in their lives, knowing for sure that their relinquished baby is now growing into a happy, adjusted adult.

Linda Todd

A Mother's Perspective

Practically forever;
I waited,
traveled through
a myriad of dark days
and nights, beyond a vast ocean.
You came to me on
that perfect day—
warm sunshine,
cloudless, sapphire sky
and golden moon,
at night.
At once,
through smiles and tears,
I recognized you
as my own.
Every day since
you found me,
I have gratefully worn
your love;
adorned with
your kisses, sweet;
bathed in salty tears,
wrapped in warm hugs....
(even covered in stickers!)

You tickle me
with giggles,
delighted laughter,
constant inquiries (about
everything and nothing at all!)
and music of sweet voices singing,
"I love you's"
each morning.
Your smiles
melt me like sunshine,
your contented gaze, and
my day complete.
At night,
a peaceful moon
and stars
watch over our
contented slumber
of a dream come true.
My little angels, you teach me much,
but most of all—
the multitude of wonders
I missed, before
I belonged to you.

Lisa Wooden Chalice

Only one year ago, I was awaiting a priceless Fed-Ex delivery—our Ukrainian travel visas—while I packed and unpacked the multitude of borrowed suitcases and travel paraphernalia that were strewn about my house. My husband, John, and I were about to travel to Ukraine to adopt our children, yet we knew nothing about them. In my "expectant mother" dreams, I often fantasized about a little boy; I guess I had to imagine some sweet angel who might occupy the bedroom we had so painstakingly prepared.

After the months of waiting—our visas, then our departure date arrived so quickly we scarcely had time to finish packing. On a Monday afternoon, we arrived in Kyiv, Ukraine. The next morning, we awoke to undertake our first order of business, an interview at the adoption center in Kyiv. We arrived early at a modest building that did nothing to foretell the important events that would take place inside. As we climbed several flights of stairs, I felt we would never reach the top. Breathless, I peered down the empty, dimly lit corridor, at the end of which was the office of the adoption center director. We stood outside in the cold hallway, shivering, until she was ready for us. The director greeted us in a friendly, yet business-like manner; I felt so nervous that I immediately forgot the greeting I had practiced in Ukrainian. As dismal as the corridor had been, her office was surprisingly bright and cheerful, with fresh flowers on the table where we sat, and photos of adopted children proudly displayed.

After a brief interview, another adoption center employee showed us photos of available children. Our translators read us each child's information, which was scanty, at best, and the photos were two or three years old. Once we selected a child to meet, the director handed us a second photo and suggested we meet this child as well. (As it happened, that child is now our daughter, Olena.) We waited in the icy-cold corridor again, for the letter giving us permission to travel to the Cherkasy region. Once we had the letter, we were on our way to Cherkasy where our children were waiting!

What we hoped for, but did not yet realize—we were one day away from meeting our forever children: Olena, Lina, and Vlady. Cherkasy is approximately two and a half to four hours south of Kyiv by car, depending on weather or how safely your driver can pass the multitude of slow-moving trucks and bicyclists on the narrow, two-lane highway. It was a veritable obstacle course—as if the prospect of meeting our children for the first time was not enough to fill my stomach with butterflies.

We drove past Cherkasy Children's Home #1 that evening. We had dinner and tried to get some rest at our hotel. The next day would be October 27. I think my impressions from my journal describe it best.

> A rooster is crowing so it must be time to get up. It seemed to begin crowing at 7 AM. I have been awake since nearly 6 AM. This is the second time I've felt cold in Ukraine, and both times have been indoors (the first time was in the corridor of the adoption center). I crouched in the shower this morning, hugging myself for some warmth, because I was so terribly nervous and frozen. I was glad to get it over with so

I could stop shivering . . . I think today is the day we will meet our children.

The orphanage is nestled in a residential area, along the Dnipro River. You drive down a narrow, bumpy road with houses on both sides and then there is the orphanage. The buildings look new and there is playground equipment, mostly monkey bars. It is sad to think they had to build such a place, but I am thankful for it if our children are there, waiting for us. . . .

"We have to dress up again today. We will go to the Cherkasy City Hall, to the Board of Education, and to the Children's Home after that. My tummy does not feel so great this morning. . . . So far I have eaten most things because I have been so hungry. . . . I think I am experiencing the most culture shock here. No matter how much Ukrainian blood is flowing through my veins, Cherkasy seems like another universe.

It was a mild October day; a soft carpet of fallen leaves covered the ground. When we arrived at the orphanage, we walked through the iron gates, and through the doors of the orphanage for the first time—my stomach was doing cartwheels. There was a group of small children walking with a caregiver to a play area. Near the heavy front door, a cat was looking at us and purring cautiously. Just inside was a set of stairs going up in opposite directions. We entered the director's office and sat in front of her desk, not facing her, but facing sideways—an arrangement that would become familiar in time. After meeting with her, we walked to a bright, spacious room on the upper level. As we entered the room, I was more emotional than I expected to be. We met three children, one of whom is now our oldest daughter, Olena, the same girl we had seen in a three-year-old black-and-white photo at the adoption center. We decided against adopting the other two boys we met. It sounds unbelievable, but I fell in love with Olena instantly, though I knew little about her. As she played with toys, she always made sure she kept me in view. There was a minor problem—we desired a sibling group, and she had no siblings. Later that same day, we watched Olena practice for an autumn dance recital. There we spotted her future sister, Lina, and brother, Vlady. We fell for them just as hopelessly as we had with Olena. John and I looked at each other later that evening, knowing that the idea of three children had been a contingency plan, in case there was a sibling group of three, but we knew these children were our children now. There was no longer a problem—Olena would now have two siblings! It would certainly not be easy, but no other solution was possible—we loved them already.

I later wrote: "Today I met my kids. I think that sentence says more than I could write in a book; MY KIDS—those have to be the two most beautiful words in the English language. MY KIDS . . . I will say it over and over again until I believe it myself."

I can find no words to describe with any accuracy, that moment when my children entered my life forever. The caregivers brought Olena in first. I can still hear her footsteps as she came through the doorway of the room where we were waiting. Without hesitating, she hurled her slender body across the wooden floor and into mine. She slammed into me so hard she knocked the wind right out of me, and then her body seemed to melt into me and there are no more words to say after that, only tears. There she was, almost four feet tall, sweating in her red snow pants. No matter how heavy she felt or how much we both sweated, she kept her soft, small cheek pressed tightly against mine and ran her fingers through my hair as if to make sure I was real. My two younger children, Lina and Vlady, entered my life in similar fashion. If I had had any doubt, their embraces dispelled it. I went back to our hotel that night dreaming of their sweet, happy faces.

From that day on, we visited our children daily, often twice a day for two more weeks. We spent hour upon hour playing with them on the wooden floors of the orphanage. We ran and played with them outside in the play yard, and began teaching them English. The days passed slowly, and I was beginning to get very homesick. We had experienced some nice autumn weather when we first arrived, but by now winter was setting in.

Finally, we had our court date on November 12 and the days went by quickly again as we made preparations to return home to Michigan. It was a bitterly cold, snowy day in Kyiv when we finally boarded the plane to Warsaw. A few days and a couple of embassies later, we arrived home in the wee hours of Thanksgiving morning—weary, jet-lagged, but relieved to be home at last. As difficult as it was, I know every Thanksgiving from now on will hold special meaning for our family. We have *much* to be thankful for. We are a family at last!

What God Has Joined Together: A Family in Process

Kisses in the Wind
(The Waiting Child's Lullaby)

I hold you in my heart and touch you in my dreams.
You are here each day with me, at least that's how it seems.

I know you wonder where we are . . . what's taking us so long.
But remember child, I love you so and God will keep you strong.

Now go outside and feel the breeze and let it touch your skin . . .
Because tonight, just as always, I blow you kisses in the wind.

May God hold you in His hand until I can be with you.
I promise you, my darling, I'm doing all that I can do.

Very soon, you'll have a family for real, not just pretend.
But for tonight, just as always, I blow you kisses in the wind.

May God wrap you in His arms and hold you very tight.
And let the angels bring the kisses that I send to you each night.

Pamela Durkota
(written for Josh)

When I was a young teen, I often told my mother when I married I was going to adopt children at three years of age so they would already be potty trained and I would not have to deal with diapers. She would counter with "you'll need to clear that with your wife." Thirty years later, I find that my plan had no basis in reality—I had a four- and five-year-old in diapers for almost a year. But I am getting ahead of myself.

Although my wife, Lisa, and I had first discussed adoption with each other twenty-one years ago, even before we were engaged, we didn't actually contact an adoption agency for six years after our wedding. We were living in Queens in New York at the time, and decided to check out an agency in New Jersey. We were very discouraged by our fact-finding mission. The counselor we met with told us we were looking at a three- to five-year wait for a white baby. We told her we were open to other ethnic groups, but were told we did not qualify. Even though Lisa's grandfather was Cuban, she did not have a Hispanic maiden name; therefore, since neither of us could prove Hispanic heritage, we could not adopt a Hispanic child. The same was the case for a black or bi-racial child. The greatest obstacle though was their fee: $15,000 or 20 percent of our annual gross income, whichever was greater. Since their fee would have taken almost half our income, that particular door had definitely closed.

It was ten years ago that Lisa and I started to actively pursue adoption. We had recently left New York and purchased our first home—a two-bedroom condo—and wanted to fill it with children. I was sure there was a way to adopt on our budget, so we filled out an application with the South Carolina Department of Social Services. We knew it might take a while, but still didn't have the $10,000–$15,000 most of the private agencies we inquired with were asking for.

Once our application was completed, we started taking adoption classes. We were a little nervous when our home study was scheduled during the middle of a construction project in the house. The social worker put us at ease almost instantly. We spent over two hours talking, and she never left the living room. When she left, we thought "Wow! This might actually happen!" Sadly, our excitement didn't last long. The weeks without a call became months and then a year with no call.

We looked for ways to keep our hopes alive. We considered going to India to adopt. (We knew an Indian evangelist whose father had government connections. He was sure if we could get there, a few calls would have us leaving with the child of our choice.) Once again, cost was a barrier. When we did hear from DSS, (Department of Social Services) it was not quite what we expected. They asked if we would be willing to become foster parents for their new foster-to-adopt program. That was fine with us as long as we were only placed with "adoptable" children. We started shopping for a crib "knowing" it would soon be filled. Still no call came.

After waiting almost two years from our home study, we decided to take our lives off hold. We bought a house with a park off the backyard (still looking hopefully to the future). We planned a vacation to Mexico and secured non-refundable airline tickets. That must have been the secret formula. Three months after moving, and two weeks after scheduling our trip, we received the long-awaited call—DSS had a four-week-old girl and wanted to know if we were we interested. We were instructed to take some time to think about it and call the following morning to give them our decision. Like there was any chance we would decline.

We had five days to prepare for our new baby while dealing with the emotional roller coaster adoption is. We would go from overwhelming joy (We're getting a baby!) to disbelief (This isn't really happening.) to something akin to terror (What if we are bad parents? How can we afford this? What if they change their minds once we get her?). But after five days of being physically and emotionally drained, we nervously joined our caseworker to go meet and bring home our daughter.

Being first-time parents brings many new challenges, and doing it at thirty-five doesn't make it any easier. After enjoying eleven years as a couple, we had to restructure how we functioned as a family. I took the night feeding shifts, more out of self-preservation than any conscious effort to be a considerate husband. The few times Lisa got up to feed Juliana, she would bring her back to our room and talk to her for about an hour, assuring I wasn't getting sleep either. I could usually get her fed and back to bed in half that time and actually get some sleep.

After a grueling five weeks as new parents, we took a much-deserved vacation. Ok, it was the non-refundable trip we had booked two months earlier. We wanted to take Juliana with us, but were certain we would have problems with customs trying to bring her back into the country with no papers on her. We managed to enjoy our brief getaway between calls to Grandma to check on her.

For years we had heard how children "control" what the family does. We were determined not to let that happen. Juliana took her first vacation at eighteen weeks when we took a fourteen-hour road trip to upstate New York. Six weeks later, she went on her first camping trip. Aside from setting up a new tent for the first time, in the dark and in the rain, it went really well. Juliana slept through the thunder while Lisa and I played mancala on the floor.

We did make some adjustments as we settled into being a family of three. There was less money to do things, and spontaneity took more planning, but Juliana kept up with our schedule. In fact, we were doing so good as parents that when Juliana was about fourteen months old, we started talking about our second child. We contacted Christian Family Services, a local adoption agency, made them a profile, and started filling out an application. While we considered whether to proceed, we got a call from our former DSS caseworker. Someone had asked her if we were still in the system because she could not find our name. She needed an adoptive home for an eighteen-month-old boy, Justice. We leapt into action, updating our home study and filling out the necessary paperwork to reactivate our file with DSS adoptions.

We did everything they asked and waited for the call to go and pick up our son. His picture and profile were faxed to us, fueling our impatience. Lisa went out and bought a boy sippy cup for his anticipated arrival. Juliana asked whom it was for. We told her it was for her brother, who hadn't come yet. We talked with our caseworker weekly to see what was happening—after all, they asked for us specifically. After a couple months, we were getting a little discouraged. Finally, about six months after we first heard about Justice we received word that he had been adopted by his foster family. We tried to console ourselves with words like, "he already knows them, so it's probably better." That did little to lessen our disappointment.

For the next few months, Lisa and I discussed what to do next. She wanted to go back to CFS (Christian Family Service). I didn't think we could afford an agency adoption and wanted to keep trying with DSS. What we did agree on was that Juliana, now two years old, needed a sibling, and we prayed we would have another child before she turned three. Lisa updated our profile and, in spite of my protests over the cost, had our CFS file activated.

Less than a week after we received our updated application package, we received a call from our caseworker, Joanne. She had just met with a young woman, Sally, six weeks from delivery who wanted a home for her baby. Joanne had taken our profile with five or six others even though we hadn't completed our application. Our profile was the third one Sally looked at. She wasn't even half way through it when she put it down and told Joanne she didn't need to go any further; she had found her baby's family.

Sally wanted to know if we would meet with her. It was not a condition of choosing us, but meant a lot to her. We had lunch with Sally and Joanne a week later. She asked what we wanted to name our soon-to-be daughter. She was making a memory book for her and wanted to spell her name correctly. When we told her we had chosen Natalia in part to honor her heritage (the birth father is Mexican) and because of the meaning (God's precious gift of joy), she almost cried.

After lunch, Sally told Lisa she could call and chat if she wanted. They spoke a couple times on the phone. Lisa started feeling a little uneasy about the "connection" that was developing, but was even more unnerved when Sally stopped accepting her calls. We later heard through Joanne that Sally was feeling uneasy too.

Things seemed to be humming along. We were working out a payment plan with CFS and securing our FMLA (Family Medical Leave Act) time in anticipation of Natalia's arrival. Then three weeks prior to our expected due date, we received word that the birth father, who had been absent for the entire pregnancy, had found out about Natalia and was threatening to take her to Mexico for his parents to raise! *This isn't supposed to happen!* we thought. *She is our baby; he has no right!* Well, technically he did, but we were not giving up without a fight. Our attorney encouraged us to proceed with placement as soon as possible after birth to strengthen our claim on her.

Most of our friends and family prayed with us for a speedy resolution.

Of course we did get a few of the obligatory pseudo-supportive comments. "Maybe this is God's way of telling you 'no.'" "Can you really afford another child?" "Wouldn't she really be better off with her biological family, even if it is the grandparents?" We thank God daily we had the courage to persevere.

Sally had wanted Lisa to be in the birthing room for Natalia's delivery. Lisa wasn't too sure she was up for that. When we got the call that Sally had gone into labor, we dashed off for the hospital still debating whether Lisa should be in on it. Thankfully that choice was made for us; Natalia was delivered a few minutes before we arrived. The midwife had just finished cleaning her, and insisted I put on her first diaper. I cautiously complied, careful not to break the tiny thing in front of me.

I don't believe I have been in a more awkward situation before or since. Sally insisted Lisa and I hold Natalia, so we sat there with her for probably forty-five minutes wanting to focus all our attention on our new baby while knowing we could not ignore the woman a few feet from us who gave us this most precious gift.

The hospital gave us a room for the night so we could stay there with Natalia. I really wanted to go home and try to get just one more good night's sleep, but that wouldn't come for several weeks. (The sleep, not home.) We left early the next morning to tend to Juliana, who had no clue what had transpired over night, and give Sally some time alone with Natalia per her request.

We returned that evening with Juliana so she could meet her new sister before we brought her home. Seconds after we entered Sally's room, a man appeared in the doorway asking to see her alone. We spent the next thirty minutes in the hall praying for no confrontation with the birth father. (We thought that it was he and this was confirmed later.) Juliana and I saw him approach the elevator. He looked at us briefly, smiled at Juliana, and left. Sally told us later he just wanted to see Natalia, and had decided not to contest the adoption; however, he would not sign any legal documents, so we still had to have the court terminate parental rights.

Juliana was thrilled to meet her new sister. When Natalia started fussing, she tried to give her a teddy bear. She asked who Sally was and why was she in bed. We explained as best we could to a two-year-old that Sally was the woman who gave birth to Natalia and was giving her to us. Upon hearing that, Juliana walked over to Sally, gave her the teddy bear (which Natalia didn't have much interest in), and said "Thank you." The three adults in the room choked up. We stayed for about another hour, and then headed home to prepare for Natalia's homecoming.

We arrived at the hospital around 8:00 AM the next morning. Lisa had brought an outfit for Natalia to come home in. Sally was having a rough time when we got there, so discharge took longer than expected. Since Natalia was born in North Carolina and we were adopting in South Carolina, the hospital could not release Natalia to us. Sally held her until the nurse wheeled her out the front door, then the nurse picked her up and handed her to me. She was really ours!

We all went back to the Christian Family Service office to sign all the papers which could not legally have been done in the hospital in North Carolina. We waited outside for a few minutes for Sally to compose herself. Once we entered the office, we took a few pictures with Sally and Natalia, and gave her some alone time to say her final good-bye. When we finally headed home, I told Lisa I didn't want to do that again—be with a birth mother during her very emotional farewell.

Being veteran parents by this time, we thought we knew what to expect with a new baby. I told Lisa I was giving her fair warning that at some point in the next few days I would "lose it" due to sleep deprivation. She just laughed it off. Needless to say we were both caught a bit off guard when I had a major meltdown a mere three hours later. Natalia refused to sleep if she wasn't being held. I was determined to let her cry herself to sleep, but could not find anywhere in the house where I could not hear her. We took turns not sleeping, trying to catch up on the other's shift.

Natalia did not handle her first road trip very well. She was about three weeks old when we pulled an all-nighter to New York. She fussed for about half of the fourteen-hour drive. Fortunately by her second road trip, twenty-six hours to Minnesota, she was sleeping through the night and seemed to enjoy the drive when she was awake.

When Natalia was about fourteen months old, we received a call from CFS. Sally was expecting again and hoped we would want another child. This was sooner than we had intended to have another baby, but the thought of Natalia actually growing up with a biological half-sibling and our concern for the baby, spurred us into action. We updated our home study and background check, started picking out names (we settled on Gabriella), and waited for the call. When we received a call from our attorney, we thought "Oh no, not again!" As it turned out, Sally had promised her baby to another agency before contacting us. I was instantly concerned about what sort of contractual/legal claim they would have. Both CFS and out attorney told us not to worry, so we cautiously waited for the right call.

That call never came. The call we did get was very disappointing. Joanne had lost contact with Sally; she was not returning calls. Joanne happened to see Sally's birth announcement in a local paper and went to the hospital to find out what was going on. She arrived as Sally was leaving with Gabriella. (We don't know what Sally named her, but that is how we will always remember her.) When Joanne confronted her, she said her sister convinced her to keep the baby even though she had no job, no home, and possible legal problems with the other agency. Disappointment doesn't even come close to what we were feeling, but we were powerless to do anything. I did call our foster contact in case Gabriella was taken into custody for any reason, but that was a long shot.

Two months after this, we went to Florida to spend a few days with Mark and Becky, friends from Minnesota who had just been placed with their second child from Bundle of Hope in Jacksonville. Becky wanted us to meet Glenda, the director of the agency, whose first question for us was: "How soon can you be ready to be placed with a baby?" My response—immediately. (Our home study had been updated three months earlier.) She said she had a baby due in four weeks, and proceeded to give us an application to complete.

Jadon was actually born five weeks later. Glenda called on Monday to let us know he had been born the night before and expected him to be released Wednesday morning, so Tuesday morning we loaded the van and headed for Florida. Shortly after checking out of the hotel Wednesday morning, we got a call from Glenda—we had a major snag. The birth mother tested positive for an STD during pregnancy, so the doctor had decided to put Jadon on penicillin as a precaution against an infection he showed no signs of having. As a result, the state of Florida would not let Jadon leave the state until his ten-day regimen was complete. Our choices were going home for a week or staying in Jacksonville and trying to get him released while we waited for his shots to end. When we told friends at work the situation, they "decided" we should stay and several sent money to cover our unexpected additional expenses. What a blessing!

We headed to the hospital while Glenda made calls to get Jadon released and find us more appropriate lodging than a hotel room for nine more days. The girls could only look at Jadon through a window while

Lisa and I went in one at a time to hold and feed him. Lisa would have spent the whole day at the hospital, but with a three-year-old and an eighteen-month-old to consider, we only stayed for about an hour before going in search of toddler entertainment, which was found at a local mall play area.

Thursday morning we checked out of our hotel and went to meet with Glenda, who was still trying to get Jadon released. We then went to the hospital again to let Jadon know we hadn't forgotten about him. Juliana stood at the window telling anyone who would listen about how Jesus gave her a baby brother and we were here to pick him up and take him home. "Do you have a baby here? There's my baby. Isn't he the prettiest baby you ever saw?"

Thursday afternoon we checked into our temporary home: a residence hotel Glenda had found for us. It was basically a small one-bedroom apartment with a kitchenette. The girls were thrilled to have their own TV, and we appreciated being able to cook instead of eating out for the entire time. It was also nice to have somewhere besides the van for naptime.

Friday morning, after making the girls their favorite breakfast (pancakes) we headed back to Glenda's office to see what was going on. Much to our great relief, she informed us Jadon was being released that evening as long as we could get a nurse to come to the hotel daily for his shots. We went to the hospital to give Jadon the good news and spent a couple hours with him before looking for some outdoor activity for the girls.

We met Glenda at the hospital around six that evening and went up to finally claim our son. We spent Saturday showing him off to some friends who came up from Port Charlotte, Florida, to celebrate with us. On Sunday, we joined Glenda at church so she could show us off to her pastor. Juliana was a bit concerned that Glenda was holding Jadon too long. She tugged on her skirt and calmly stated, "That's my brother. You can't keep him." Five days later we were free to come home.

Shortly after Jadon's first birthday, we reactivated our adoption file with DSS. We continued to take in foster children while we waited to be placed with our next child. We would check the COAC (Council on Adoptable Children) website regularly and expressed interest in individual children or sibling groups at least once a month. When we finally received the call, it came from out of the blue. A caseworker had a sister and brother who were not legally free at that point and as such had not yet made it to the COAC site. Of course we would take them!

Alizabeth and Christopher came with a laundry list of issues. Alizabeth had just turned five, but would wet herself several times a day. Christopher was almost four, but acted more like a two-year-old than Jadon, wetting and soiling himself several times a day. (It would have been easier to deal with if there were a medical issue, but they had just not been held accountable for personal hygiene.) Both were very defiant and only spoke in one volume: *loud*!

Joanne kept assuring us everyone would understand if we couldn't handle the problems. We assured her they didn't bring anything we hadn't seen before with foster kids. We also told her we couldn't even entertain that as an option if we were truly committed to making these children permanent members of our family. Most importantly, God would not have brought them to us just to have us give up on them.

They have now been with us just over a year. They both know they are an important part of our family and are excited about changing their last name. A few months ago their foster caseworker, who has been involved with their case for three years, said she knows God put them in our family. We are hopeful we can finalize their adoption by the end of summer. Then we can start praying about our next child. They've all been asking when the baby is coming. Since DSS is unlikely to have an infant available for adoption, we may be visiting CFS again soon. Our next addition, though, needs to wait until we have a larger vehicle. Our current one is full. If any one has a bus you would like to donate, I'm sure we will fill it up.

Peter Bahrenburg

Heaven Sent Four

Life is not measured by the number of breaths we take, but by the moments that take our breath away.

 Our names are Tom and Sharon Wilkerson and we have been married twenty-eight years. We had two birth children, Paul and Sarah. They were a joy and pleasure for us to love and raise. They are now twenty-five and twenty-four years old. Both married and we have one grand baby so far. We homeschooled them and were very involved in homeschool co-ops. We were support group leaders and very active in their lives, always planning field trips and projects. As they were growing older and starting to think about college and marriage, we decided to become foster parents in Tennessee. We were just not ready for the "children" days to end.
 Having children at home was so rewarding and our two were such a blessing to us that we decided we wanted to help other children. We had the perfect house for taking in sibling groups. Our first placement was for three little boys. We became so attached to them it was hard to let them go at the end of six weeks. This experience broke our hearts, but we decided to continue to do foster care for two years. After that we had three little girls for six months. Once again, it was really hard to let them go, but their mother took them back and I think foster care had been a good thing for all of them. They wrote us letters and kept up with us for a while after going back home.

We later received another sibling group of five and four of them were four and under! We had them two different times and we tried to help their birth parents get their lives back together to take care of these precious children, but unfortunately they never did. And eventually someone else took these five and adopted them. At that time we didn't feel led to adopt them. Instead God had another plan in place for them. He placed them in the perfect family.

Both our birth children ended up in Missouri. One married and the other found good employment in St. Louis and later married also. We felt led to make the long trip to Missouri to live, all the while still wanting to adopt. We had wanted to for years, but it had never seemed like the right time.

Our first year in Missouri I remember Steve Green had a little video song clip, "All I want for Christmas is a Family." It showed him in the middle of a field playing the guitar and singing this song, and all these children were coming up to him. They were children who needed homes and wanted families. I would listen and watch that over and over and just cry and cry and pray that God would bring children into our lives at the right time.

We were in an apartment at that time as we had just moved, and we were in the process of looking for a home. We were so eager to become foster parents that we contacted social services. They said to wait until we got settled and moved. They told us to contact them and take classes, which we did.

We found a wonderful small house with four acres of woods and a workshop for Tom's business. It was a perfect spot to raise children, but no children were in sight yet. We just kept praying as we took the classes. We finished up in the summer and they came to do the final check of the house and finally our home study was complete after what seemed like months and months of waiting.

The social worker came and informed us of a book of available children ready for adoption. She told us that if we saw a child or sibling group that we could then submit our home study. The next day I went to the office. As I looked through the book of children I was a little disappointed as there were no pictures only descriptions in there, such as age and a little information about them. My husband Tom and I wanted at least three boys and I wanted a girl or two. We had always wanted a large family and could only have two biologically, so this seemed like the perfect time to get a family of four.

There they were! The only thing the description said was, tree boys with blonde hair and blue eyes and a girl, all nine and under. I got so excited I told my husband and he said go for it. I quickly wrote the social worker and got a picture. We just thought and prayed, "lord, your will be done for us and these children. If these are the ones, please open the door for us to get them."

The social worker submitted the home study to an area about six hours away and they called us for an interview a month or so later, we had never been to one. We went for the staffing and they had just interviewed another couple before us. As we saw them leave we thought "Oh no they are a lot younger, so I am sure they won't pick us. We don't stand a chance." We left the interview and were riding in the car to go home feeling a little discouraged. All of a sudden our cell phone rang. It was the people we had just met with. They said that they had unanimously chosen us for these four children because they were a handful and they needed someone experienced for them. The best part was they didn't care about our age. We were shocked, scared, excited, and just thrilled, but a little worried too. We had a lot to do to get ready for four children, and these were four very active special needs children, who had had a lot of trouble learning and doing different things.

Two of the children had been in bad foster homes that had been shut down by the state. The other two had been in their birth home, starved and abused by drug-addicted and alcoholic parents. The little girl at three years old had only weighed fourteen pounds; she had almost died of starvation. When the children were found they were eating from the dumpster, which they did regularly.

When they were placed in foster care, they were all placed at different times and it sounded like these children had stayed in foster care way too long before they were ready for adoption. The foster home they were in had been waiting almost a year for them to be taken out to be put up for adoption. The foster parents said they had never intended to have all four, as they both had careers and didn't have the time, energy, or desire to adopt them; it seemed no one wanted to adopt that large of a sibling group. It also seemed that no one had really tried too hard to find a permanent family either, which was to our advantage.

So we arranged to meet the children, drove to the foster home with our new puppy, a German shepherd. When we drove up the four children came running out with a picture one of them had drawn and said "Are you our new parents and are you going to adopt us?" Having the puppy broke the ice—they loved dogs.

I was shocked. I stammered and stuttered and said, "We think so, if it all works out." We hugged them, talked with them, and played with them. I had brought them each a gift bag with matching shirts and a dress for the girl, some little stuffed animals, and some goodies. They loved that. Their teeth had been rotten so their foster parent had needed to have a lot of dental work done for them and they already had lots of caps on their teeth.

They were little and skinny, but blond and adorable. The youngest was a four-year-old boy, next a six-year-old girl, an eight-year-old boy and finally a nine-year-old boy—all siblings. They were so full of energy, jumping all around and very active. They wanted to show us everything at their foster house. After one hour we left and we just felt so much love for them. We also had fear wondering, "Can we do it?" "Should we do it?" "What if we can't keep up with them, meet their needs, or help them?" "What will our parents, family, children, and church group think?" A lot of people thought we were absolutely crazy! Our parents were so worried and unsure and scared. Some people tried to talk us out of it, but we were going to follow through with God's grace and his guidance and protection.

I am so glad we didn't let anyone talk us out of it now. We told the social worker it was too far to go back and forth for visits and we had done foster care. We knew we could do it. So after our son was married and all that was over with, we planned a date and went to pick them up. We brought them home, and they have never left.

They have been with us one year and eight months. They were a legal risk and were officially adopted in August 2007. They have now been adopted nine months. We had a special adoption ceremony at our church for family and friends to celebrate with us. We had speakers, and the children sang. Then we had snacks, food, games, and a piñata. It was a wonderful time to officially, in everyone's eyes, change their names and give them memories of the start of their new life with us, the Wilkersons.

Our boy and girl, Paul and Sarah, sang a song to them called "Welcome to the Family." In the middle of the song they reached out their arms and the four children walked up and hugged their new sister and brother. There was not a dry eye in the place the children even cried. Now when the grandparents come form Virginia to see us or we go there everyone is crying when we have to separate. Our new children have become so attached to their grandparents that they are just like a part of our family. It is as if we always had them. Everyone says they look like us and we look like our children. It's pretty exciting. We have homeschooled them ever since we got them, and that has gone well also.

The Wilkersons

A Sister's Prayer

Therefore I say unto you, What things soever ye desire,
when ye pray, believe that ye receive them,
And ye shall have them.
St Mark 11:24

There is a special story about how our fourth child came along. I have five sisters—one older and four younger. One year they all found out that they were expecting a baby within months of each other. It was not planned. This meant that each of my sisters would be having a baby that year, except me. Everyone was excited but they were all worried that I would feel hurt and left out. So, without me knowing about it they all had a special prayer and fast that somehow I would also get a baby.

Now, if you know anything about the adoption process, you would know that it would take a miracle for us to get a baby. Not only is the adoption process long and frustrating at times, but we were not on any waiting lists nor were we at the time working through any agency. Our last baby was still well under two years old.

Well, all I can say is that sincere prayer works and that if the Lord intends to add to your family, He can certainly make that happen! One night, when I was rocking our son to sleep in the family room, I got a phone call. The person on the other end, whom I knew, asked me if my husband and I were interested in adopting another baby. I was taken by surprise and told her that I hadn't really thought of it, but was curious to hear what she had to say. My husband and I believed that if it was in the Lord's plan for us, that additional children would be sent into our home. We had always prayed that if there were more children for He would direct us and open a way for that to happen. We would be willing and grateful to welcome more children to the family. What if this was the right child and the right time? I listened to her tell me of a phone call that she had received from an old college friend who had a daughter that was looking for a good LDS family that would be interested in adopting her baby. She wasn't in a position to be able to raise the baby herself and trusted her mother to help her find a suitable home and family.

This birth grandmother called her old friend from her college days at BYU and asked for her help. During their conversation, my husband and I came to her mind and she told the grandmother about us. After finishing her story, she asked me for permission to give this family our phone number. I told her that would be fine. I then told my husband about the phone call. We prayed for help in making a decision. We soon got a phone call, and the woman on the other end asked me a few questions. She said that she was having some personal problems in her life and she was dealing with some substance abuse issues also and that she knew that she needed to make a better choice for her baby at this time than what she had to offer. She knew that she could not give this child what it needed and deserved at this time because of her lifestyle and the position that she was in.

I could tell that she loved the baby and was making a very difficult and unselfish choice. After she asked me a few questions, she got choked up and handed the phone to her mother. After a few minutes, her mother got on the phone and told me that her daughter had only recently decided to place the baby for adoption and did not feel comfortable giving it up through an agency. She wanted to know for herself that it was going to a family that she approved of. She did not want to have open, continued contact with the family, but instead wanted the peace of mind that she had made a good choice and that her baby would be in a better situation. This was important to her.

Her mother then told me that as her daughter handed her the phone, she was tearful and said, "She's the one."

As those words were spoken to me, I felt a surge of love for this unborn child that I suddenly felt would soon be ours. My heart also went out to this dear mother who loved her child enough to want better for him, even if it meant breaking her own heart. I was overwhelmed with what had just happened, but was humbly grateful for the blessing it would bring into our lives.

In less than a month from the time of that phone call we were at the hospital meeting this woman, her mother, and our new little son who we got to witness being born. I was even able to cut his umbilical cord. He was healthy, perfect, and beautiful. We loved him and began to bond with him instantly. Within twenty-four hours we were headed home to introduce him to his siblings. As we were leaving, his birth mother called after me and said, "Don't slack!"

Often when I feel weary and things get difficult, as is typical in the responsibility of parenting, I recall her saying to me, "Don't slack!" and it helps me to try just a little harder. After all, she is counting on me and so is he.

So, my sisters and I *all* got a new baby that particular year. One new baby came every other month, all year. In a pattern of girl, boy, girl, boy, girl, boy. Our son came along in the very middle, keeping perfect time with the pattern. I am grateful to my sisters who prayed to the Lord in my behalf and for Him who loved me enough to give me such a priceless and unexpected gift that I value and treasure to this day.

Jona Webb

A Reason to Celebrate

As a very young child, I had an intuitive awareness that Mother's Day and Father's Day were very special. I have fond recollections of creating a "pet rock" for my dad and a macrame hanger for my mom to mark the two holidays, and remember as well "helping" my dad and two siblings prepare a Mother's Day breakfast in bed, which my mother enjoyed in spite of any shortcomings. The macaroni art projects, paintings, home-made greeting cards, and coupon booklets promising special chores, all had special significance. After all, moms and dads were special people and deserved to be honored. How simple it all was. Almost as natural as breathing.

Many years later, when I married and looked forward to becoming a mother myself, Mother's Day was still a day to honor my mother. But it was also a day that filled me with hope of what was to come. I knew that it would soon be my turn to be a parent and share my life with a child or children of my own. As time went by, however, Mother's Day became a milestone, marking each childless year as it passed. The grief and loss I felt were profound, but in retrospect, they helped me gain a valuable perspective the made me more appreciative of what I had and made me understand that motherhood and fatherhood are precious gifts. I learned, through not having a child, what an awesome honor and privilege it is to be responsible for a child and to love a child, whether or not I was the one who brought him or her into this world.

The most humbling experience of being an adoptive parent is to be entrusted with the future of another mother's child. In my case, there are three beautiful young lives that remind me every day that this is the most important job I will ever have. And though I did not attain motherhood in the traditional manner, my role as a mother gives me many compelling reasons to feel special and to celebrate Mother's Day.

The first Mother's Day with my three children had a dream-like quality. It was a lovely spring day and I had been a mother for six whole months. My children were five, six, and seven at the time, and having just emigrated from Ukraine half a year earlier, they had no idea what Mother's Day in America meant. As their adoptive mother, how could I have imagined what this day really meant, for me or for my children? My first mistake was in thinking that Mother's Day was *my* day. I could not have been more mistaken.

Sitting in church that Mother's Day morning, my children fidgeted as I dreamed of the beautiful red carnation—the once illusive symbol of motherhood—that would be mine at the end of liturgy. I was now entitled to possess it, and I strolled proudly up the center aisle of the church in my brand new Mother's Day attire to claim my prize. My children, who always clung to me and would not risk letting me out of their sight for a moment, followed me. And at the front of the church, as *all* of us received blessed flowers from the priests, I realized that it was not *my* day after all. I was overlooking something very important.

Following the church service, my husband took us to a Mother's Day brunch. My children misbehaved. They picked at their food, whined, squirmed, and were quite disagreeable. They couldn't have cared less about this brunch, let alone this day. I tried to make the most of the situation, but in the end, it was a day no one enjoyed—least of all me. My first Mother's Day was nothing like what I had imagined it would be, and perhaps it was unrealistic and even a little selfish of me to have had such high expectations.

My children and I had openly discussed their birth parents, even when communication had been quite a challenge. When they first became our children, their birth mother was "druha mama"—the other mother—and I understood them well enough to know that they missed her and loved her. And yet, on this Mother's Day, I had neglected to acknowledge the mothers who were so conspicuously absent. And while my intentions were good and my heart was filled with an abundance of love for my new children and a great joy at having become their mother, I had forgotten something. I had viewed the day as something due me—a birthright coveted at the expense of everything else.

My perspective on Mother's Day has changed from what it was that first idealistic year. In truth, it is still evolving. And as difficult as it has been for me to deal with such disappointments, I have come to understand that my children were grieving on this day of celebration, grieving for the loss of all things familiar—their birth parents, birth country, their caregivers, and their friends. Considering this, it is not surprising that they were less than enthusiastic about celebrating a day called Mother's Day with someone who was, in so many ways, a stranger.

Because of this strangeness, every one of us viewed that first Mother's Day from a different perspective and, unfortunately, our expectations based on those viewpoints did not mesh. After two years together, we are still strangers in many ways. Some days my children are not even sure if they like me all that much. They have no control over anything that has happened to them in their short lives, and now they face yet another Mother's Day with me, without ever having said good-bye to their birth mothers. How brave these little souls must be to face their grief amid the expectations of this special day.

This year will mark my fourth Mother's Day. It looms somewhat ominously, like a spring storm. There is no telling how much rain we will get. Now that my children are in school, Mother's Day is not just one simple day—it is more like an entire season. At school, there will be events honoring all mothers; my children are excited to be involved in doing something special for me, yet the world they live in has no wonderful party planned to remember the mothers who gave them life, a mother they miss and sometimes hate because she is not part of their lives.

This Mother's Day, I am looking forward to wearing my favorite pin. It is a beautiful gold-colored Winnie-the-Pooh pin, given to me by a dear friend. It says "Mom." When I pin it to my dress, I will smile, because this is who I am now. This year, I am looking forward to celebrating what is most amazing about my motherhood: growing in love and wisdom and building a relationship with my three children in spite of all the obstacles we face. Our brief time together has not always been blissful, but it has been in all ways miraculous. I plan to enjoy this Mother's Day, whatever it may bring and however stormy it may be. And this year I will not forget to acknowledge the women who brought them into this world.

I do not know how Mother's Day 2003 will turn out, but I am certain that it will begin very early in the morning. There will be many wet, doggie-breath kisses from the golden retrievers pouncing on me until they are certain I am awake. If I am lucky, there will be breakfast, or least coffee, in bed. From my children, there are sure to be smiles, hugs and kisses, beautiful handmade greeting cards, school projects, and many other surprises. Sitting here tonight, reflecting on past Mother's Days and looking forward to new ones, I can't complain.

Lisa Calice

On the Occasion of Our First Year Together and Thanksgiving

Tonight you professed your love to me with
small arms wrapped tightly about my neck
"Mama, I love you so much" and blinking back happy tears,
"I love you too".
After I closed bedroom doors you slept and dreamed a child's dream
while I marveled at the fairy-tale-like vision of
half-a-dozen little shoes lined up near my door.
I gulped a breath of air and amazement and wondered,
in your night's dreams do you see the life you have given me?

On this day, you and me have been "WE" a whole year!
And yet, I still marvel at your existence.
Well-thought-out plans and dreams, the parent I would be,
what I would teach you in a year's time—surprise!
All thrown to the wind.
You taught ME.

Because of you, our pasts,
I learned never to forget:
what it was like to not be a blessed mom to
three precious children, or
what neither of us had before we met.

I learned to love those radiant smiles of yours

where your eyes light up with joy; that for me
is like peering into the sun.
Sweet melody of your voices, like a chorus of angels singing,
and your cherubic faces beam with your affection;
feel silken next to mine, and I
learned to rejoice in the awesome splendor
that is your love.

Grinning, you asked me this morning,
"Open presents today, Mama?"
And memories swept me swiftly back to a year ago
when you still wore those too-big sweaters
and smelled pungently of kasha and cabbage.
In your innocence, you thought a balloon
from a first visit to McDonald's was a "gift,"
and in mine, I believed it
not impressive enough to win your affection.
A year later, in your sleep of contentment
the only worthy gift for you is me.

Again and again, in this year gone by,
I pondered this great miracle,
cherished the remarkable joy of your devotion
when you tugged me close for extra hugs, your small
child's bodies securely melted into mine
curled up in my lap of your contentment, just because . . .
because we have "US!"
Countless times I stole silently into your room at night
under guise of duty
just to watch your peaceful sleep and
listen to you breathe starry night air,
like sweet angels who on a divine mission
stopped to slumber here with me.
How is it of all possibilities—you chose me?

In hush of sun-filled morning, I will sip coffee in
quiet solitude, gazing in awe through a window of world

forever altered by your arrival
full of hope as I await welcome rhythm
of three sets of little feet hurrying down the stairs
to greet me with first kiss of day.
Somewhere in warm embraces and flurry of
"I love you's," I will find a few tears of joy on my cheek;
"Mama, why you crying?"
"Because I love you"
my being your mama is the greatest gift of all
and I silently give thanks.

Lisa Marie Wooden Calice (11/2000)

My Destinee

As you lay sleeping far away
as still as you could be . . .
How could you know the joy today
this photo brings to me?

A few short weeks and you'll be mine,
and "I" will soon be "We."
How could you know the love I feel?
It's something you can't see.

So have sweet dreams, my precious babe.
Sleep well and tenderly.
Some say that you're the lucky one.
How could you know it's me?

Kris Laughlin

Our adoption story starts like many I am sure. My husband and I are unable to have children. We tried for years and we were unsuccessful. We went through a lot of treatments and it just got to be too much for me. We settled on the idea of adoption.

We had some friends who adopted through DFCS (Department of Family and Children's Services) and after much discussion we decided that was the route for us. We went to an Adoption Party sponsored by the state. We went looking for a younger child. We knew the odds of finding one at the party were slim. The party was great; it was set up so there were seven different stations. Each station had an activity. The directors of the party told us to just have fun and play with the children. They asked us to not ask them a lot of questions. As soon as we saw Destinee we knew she destined to be our child. She was twelve—older then we original wanted—but that did not matter. She has this smile that blows people away. We played some games with her and ate some pizza. She was all tomboy. There was another couple also interested in Destinee. They also spent some time with her. As we started to leave I told Destinee good-bye but I hoped we would be seeing her soon. As we got into the car I looked at my husband and asked him what he thought. He said he knew she was meant to be our daughter. As soon as we got home I called DFCS in Henry County, Georgia. All I got for days was an answering machine. I told my husband, "They are not calling us back because they have already chosen the other couple." My husband was not worried. He already knew that God meant for Destinee to come live with us.

Soon DFCS did call back; they had received our home study and were sending information about Destinee to our local DFCS. They asked us to go over it. They said if we changed our minds after we learned about Destinee that there would still be time to back out.

Our caseworker called us in and went over Destinee's history. We learned she had been given up by her mother because her mother could not handle her. Destinee has other brothers and sisters and the mother kept all of them. Destinee was told by her mother that is she were a better girl they would have kept her. She had it in her mind that it was her fault she was not with her family. She had a list of mental problems. After about an hour the caseworker finished telling us everything we needed to know about Destinee. We looked at her and said, "So when can we began visitations with her?" We didn't care about the problems. We strongly felt that if we got her home we could work on the problems.

We began visitations with her the next month. The first visit was in her town. The next couple of visits we brought her to our home. After four months we were finally able to bring her home for good. It took us sixteen months to get the adoption finalized. It has not been easy. Destinee is not one who trusts adults in her life easily. She and I have had more problems than with her dad. Destinee does not trust women, so I have really had to work with her. She has been a blessing to us and has made us a family. It has been two years and Destinee has blossomed into a normal teenage girl. She loves sports, music, and being outside. She is still somewhat of a tomboy, but I do catch glances of a girl under there sometimes. She has a big heart but she tries to hide it. I am so proud to call her my daughter. Lately we have been talking about adopting again. We are making sure Destinee is involved in the process—she is ready to be a sister again.

Rebecca Cason

Adoption—It's All About Love

And the Lord, he it is that doth go before thee;
he will be with thee; He will not fail thee,
neither forsake thee: fear not; neither be dismayed.
Deuteronomy 31:8

I just thought that I would share a few personal thoughts on adoption. There is a little poem that I love. (I don't know the author.)

> Not flesh of my flesh nor bone of my bone, but still miraculously my own.
> Never forget for a single minute, that you didn't grow under my heart,
> But *in* it.

Growing up I certainly never considered that adoption would play such a profound role in my life! Both my husband and I came from large families. I have one sister that has thirteen children and one that has twelve. My husband's siblings also all have large families. I had no thoughts one way or the other about adoption before I became involved with it. Now I have very strong, and also very tender feelings regarding this wonderful blessing called adoption. If not for adoption, I would not have five wonderful children who bring me such joy and happiness. They give my life greater purpose and have fulfilled the life-long desire I had to be a mother, have a family, and experience all the blessings, struggles, and rewards that can only come through parent/child relationships.

As I learned of my infertility issues, I was very disappointed. I felt deep sorrow in the fact that one of my fondest dreams—that of being a mother—might never be realized. It left a void that *nothing* else could replace. As wonderful as other things could be, they could never take the place of having a child of our own to love and nurture. My maternal instincts were strong and could not be dismissed. Once I realized that it might never be possible for me to conceive and bear a child, I was heartbroken, but I wasn't willing to give up! My heart yearned and ached for a child, and although I would have welcomed the experience of pregnancy and childbirth, I was less concerned about *how* my children would come to me, and more concerned that they just come! From the start I never looked at adoption as a last resort or a lesser option. I just looked at it as a different way for the Lord to bring our children into our lives, our home, and our family. I believed that He had an ultimate design and plan for me as well as for everyone else.

As I anticipated the arrival of each child, I had the same hopes and excited anticipation as any other mother. I just didn't have an exact time frame or date to plan on. It may have not been the natural process of getting them here, but once I held them in my arms, I knew they were my babies and I loved them instantly. The bond was definitely there. My joy was overflowing and the prayers of my heart were answered. I was a mother. Some may say that I wasn't their "real mother," but I say that for me the feelings were as real as anything that I had ever felt. I didn't see them as adopted. I saw them as a gift from God, as are all children. I don't understand all of the reasons why I was not able to have children in the traditional way, but I am grateful that regardless of the difficulties, they did come and they are here and they are the sweetest part of my life. I wish that I could say that I have done everything right as a mother, but just like any other mother, I have a few regrets along the way. Parenting is on-the-job training, after all.

If given a second chance we all could and would do things better, but one thing I do know is that I have loved my children with the kind of special love that only exists between a mother and child. Each one has enriched my life and I cannot imagine what it would have been like for me without them. They are so important to me and I still feel such gratitude for them. I feel thankful to their birth mothers who loved and cared for them enough to break their own hearts in order to choose a more stable life for their children. It must have been the hardest thing they have ever had to do! I have kept them in my prayers through the years and have special feelings in my heart regarding them. We share something very special between us. Their courage to make an unselfish choice provided me the opportunity of a lifetime and I will never forget their sacrifice. Thank you. Bless you, birth mothers.

Another saying that I love is: "Adoption—it's all about love." It is love that motivates us to open our hearts, our arms, and our lives and be a part of such a beautiful experience. Our family may not have all come about in the normal way, but we are a real family with the real ups and downs that all families face, and we really do love each other. It just doesn't get more *real* than that. I don't feel that we were put together by chance or by accident. I believe in a master plan. We now have two beautiful grandchildren who expand our circle of love. In our home, the word "adoption" is a positive thing. It is the process through which our family was brought together, and there is no greater blessing in life than families. If this is the way the Lord chose for us, then I say "thank you" and I wouldn't trade it for any other way. My children are the jewels in my crown, and as a mother, I have been richly blessed!

Jona Webb

From Russia to China

Do not be afraid, for I am with you; I will bring your
children from the east and gather you from the west.
I will say to the north, "Give them up!" and to the south,
"Do not hold them back." Bring my sons from afar
and my daughters from the ends of the earth.
Isaiah 43:5-6

The hardest part of starting my story is figuring out where to begin. There are lots of points in time—a long bike ride during a break from an ex-patriate assignment in China, during which I decided adopting from China was the right thing for me. Or maybe the long walk with my dad during which we talked about me adopting and whether I wanted a boy or a girl. Or the time that I was talking to a friend because I was frustrated by yet another failed relationship, and hearing the friend's offer of help should I decide to adopt. But I think that those are too late in time to really mark the beginning of my journey.

My story is more than just a travelogue describing my trips to China and Russia. Those stories are wonderful memories, and they are the stories of the start of my family, but they are not, in and of themselves, my entire adoption story. My adoption story started much earlier than the day, five years ago now, that my plane touched down in Moscow and I first saw the beautiful picture of my daughter Vicka.

Throughout my whole life, I really desired to be a family, and to have a happy, traditional, nuclear family. I had had long-term relationships, some of them very long-term. However, it just seemed that those relationships were never with the right people to establish a permanent family. I knew that I wanted children—I would always feel an emptiness inside and a sense of melancholy when a new family member was born or when a friend gave birth. I didn't want to diminish the joy, but it was a painful experience for me.

My career has always been important to me, and I've always been very proud of my work and my success in the workplace. I've worked in information technology my entire career. While I had always traveled as part of my work, I usually stayed in the continental United States and in Canada. In 1999 I had a chance to work overseas in Shanghai. It was a wonderful experience for me, especially since my work, while challenging, wasn't completely all absorbing and Shanghai is an interesting place to spend time.

If you had told me when I was in college that my life would look as it does today—fifty years old, a single parent with two children adopted from Russia and China, and with a daily two-hour commute and an executive-level job, I would have looked at you as though you were crazy. And the part I would have thought craziest is the single, adoptive parent stuff.

So life happened while I was making other plans. In 1999, I got the opportunity of a lifetime—to spend six months living and working in Shanghai, PRC. Once during my stay I returned to the States for a couple of business meetings. While I was home, I took my bicycle out on a trail. While riding I decided that what I wanted to do was to adopt a child. My plan at that time was to adopt from China.

I began the paperwork with an agency that I saw online. I chose them because of the founders' history with international adoption. They had literally written the book on how to adopt internationally. I put in an application and talked to a social worker.

It soon became clear to me that adoption wouldn't be an easy process. I was living in a hotel and having conversations with my agency about social workers flying in from Guam to do a home study. It wasn't the time to adopt.

After I returned from my ex-patriate assignment, I traveled for business for a couple more years. But I still wanted to have a family. I began to attend some seminars offered by various adoption agencies. I researched countries, and talked to some people who had adopted. I then began to research adoption agencies. My first step was to submit for my authorization to adopt from the INS (Immigration and Naturalization Services). I also found a local agency to do my home study.

At that point I was planning to adopt from Kazakhstan and I began to create a dossier for that adoption. However, after some long conversations with the directors of the adoption agency I had chosen, I decided to change my country to Russia. My agency suggested that I adopt from the Krasnodar region.

Although I was still traveling for work, collecting the paperwork from my dossier went very smoothly. Once everything was together, I submitted my dossier to Russia. I waited for about two months before I got a call that there was a child that met my needs in Krasnodar. Soon after, I had a travel date.

My father and I packed our bags and got on the plane to go to Moscow. We arrived in Moscow on a Saturday. Our driver met us at the airport and took us to our hotel. We would leave the next morning to fly to Krasnodar. That evening, we took a cab into Moscow proper, and had dinner at a restaurant on the edge of Red Square. I remember being amazed at Red Square and the beauty of the Kremlin.

On Sunday we got on the plane and flew to Krasnodar. It was about a two-and-a-half-hour flight from Moscow. I looked out on the Kuban Steppe from the airplane and marveled at the beautiful green countryside.

Our adoption facilitator and our driver met us at the airport. We stayed in a hotel in Krasnodar City. Our appointment with the Ministry of Education was the next morning. We walked around the city a little bit, then came home and went to bed—the next day would be a big day.

The director was late for our appointment. She asked a lot of difficult questions to make sure that I knew that being a single parent would be hard. She asked my dad if he would help me, and he promised to. She told me that she did not have any three- to four-year-old girls, but she did have some boys. Would I be interested in adopting a boy? I said no, and then she said she knew of a two-year-old girl who wanted a mother. Would I be interested in her? I said yes. She showed me a picture of a little girl on a rocking horse. "She is beautiful" I said. Before I knew it, we were in the car and on the way to meet Vicka.

The orphanage was about a two-hour drive from Krasnodar city. We drove into the orphanage and were shown into the director's office. The director talked to us about Vicka, and told us, "She is perfect." He went to get her. A few minutes later, we heard someone crying. I stepped out into the outside chamber, and there she was—my Vicka, crying.

We went outside and walked around the yard. I took her hand—she was walking well—and we looked at flowers and at some books and pictures I gave her. I left her a doll, which she held, and a blanket to sleep with. I had slept with the blanket so I could leave her something that smelled like me.

After Vicka was taken back to the room, we went to lunch. I made up my mind that Vicka would be my daughter. I signed the paperwork. We would come back in a month to bring her home.

Since the orphanage did not encourage us to stay and visit Vicka, we took a flight the next day back to Moscow. From there, we took an overnight train to St. Petersburg and spent two days wandering around. We took another overnight train back to Moscow and toured the Kremlin the next day. We returned to the States the next day.

I was very busy over the next four weeks. Getting cribs, baby proofing the house, finishing some painting, and making sure Vicka's room was ready all kept me busy. I had not said anything about the adoption to most of my co-workers, so I needed to get everyone up to speed and I needed to get ready to be gone for my three-month leave of absence.

Our return trip to Russia was exciting. My dad and I traveled first to Moscow and spent the night there. Coincidentally, the night we arrived was the night that Paul McCartney performed live in Red Square. We had a day before our flight to Krasnodar so we took a walking tour of Moscow and stopped at some markets on the street. It was interesting to learn about Moscow, but very hard to concentrate on the sighseeing, knowing that my court hearing was in a couple of days.

We traveled back to Krasnodar. This time, we stayed in a small apartment owned by a mother and sister who cooked for us. They were very hospitable. We settled down to sleep the night before the court hearing, but neither of us could sleep.

My court hearing was "in chambers" and was done with me, my dad, the facilitator, and the judge. It was Memorial Day back in the States, a Monday. With only one minor gaffe, the judge took testimonials from me, the facilitator, and the social worker I had met on my first trip. She then took a recess while we waited for her decision. A few short minutes later, we were called back into chambers and Vicka was mine!

The next day, we got into the car and went to the orphanage to get Vicka. We had a lot of paperwork to complete. After it was completed, the orphanage director picked Vicka up and held her. He showed me to her, and said, "This is your mother." When we finally were allowed to take Vicka, we took her up to the room where she had spent most of her life so that her care takers could say "good-bye." I still can see that room in my mind, with all of the children and so few caretakers.

Vicka screamed and cried when we took her into the car. She settled down when we got her some juice. We went to lunch and she sat on my lap. As soon as lunch came, she grabbed my fork from me and ate all of the peas on my plate. After a while, she decided this was an okay place to be. She ate all of her meals well. She would not let me out of her sight, and wouldn't let my dad push her stroller. She wasn't going to let me go!

When all of the paperwork was completed in her region, we flew back to Moscow. While there we ran into some other adoptive families who were watching us. They had decided that Vicka wasn't adopted because we appeared to have bonded so quickly.

We needed to take Vicka to a medical clinic before we went to the embassy to get her visa to enter the States. We had been concerned because she had a distended abdomen. The doctor told me that it was caused by rickets, which is easily cured by Vitamin D and exposure to the sun. Other than that, she was a healthy little girl who understood everything the doctor asked her to do.

Once we had Vicka's visa, we returned to the States. We had to spend the night in Amsterdam. Vicka was good on the flight from Moscow to Amsterdam. She liked to run a lot. When we got on the morning flight from Amsterdam to Detroit, the flight attendant looked at her and said, "You're a runner, aren't you." Dad was across the aisle from Vicka and I, so we could allow her to go a little way between us.

When we arrived at our final destination, my mom and Vicka's new cousin Logan were waiting for us. Her new aunt Linda and uncle Al were there as well. She would meet her new aunt Susan and cousin Erin a little later in the day.

We stayed with my mom and dad for a couple of days after we arrived home. Vicka was afraid of their Bouvier at first but she got used to him. It was a good thing because there was another Bouvier waiting at our house for her—my pet of about three years.

Vicka got used to her family very quickly. Her cousins adored her (and still do), and she adored them. She got to know the people in the neighborhood and at our church, and she was soon everyone's darling. When she had her third birthday party it was a big event because we had to celebrate three birthdays in one.

Vicka and I grew very close as she grew. She had some issues with nighttime and going to sleep, but she outgrew those. She is stubborn, but so I am. She is funny and she is a sweet girl. She is a talented athlete—especially at swimming and tennis. She is well-adjusted and intelligent.

After she had been home about two years, Vicka started asking for a sister. I think she was a bit lonely and wanted to have a playmate. I had not intended to adopt again. Being a single parent with one child was rough, but with two I knew it would be really rough. Vicka can be pretty insistent, though, and it got me thinking about what it would be like to adopt again.

As I mentioned before, I had also wanted to adopt a child from China. After I had spent some time in China, I felt a connection with the country and with the culture. The agency I liked so well no longer did Russian adoptions. I started looking into Chinese programs.

I once again began the paperwork for a dossier for China. With a small child to care for, the process took a little more time. I was able to have my paperwork hand-delivered to China by the agency's person in China, who had come to the States for the agency's twenty-fifth anniversary celebration.

I was looking at my agency's website and saw a picture of an adorable little girl on their China special needs adoption page. She had some medical issues early in life. I contacted my agency, and they sent me the paperwork on a little girl named Xing Fu Mei, who would soon become Mei Margaret or Maggie. I signed the paperwork. I knew who my daughter was going to be, I just didn't know when I was going to travel.

Fortunately, it didn't take very long. I was to travel at the end of 2006. I would travel alone, and Vicka would stay with my parents. The timing was good, because there were lots of distractions for Vicka—family gatherings for Christmas, New Years' parties, and so forth. I was able to make arrangements to travel easily.

My trip to China lasted two weeks. I met Maggie on Christmas Eve in the lobby of the Child Welfare Agency in Nanchang, Jiang Xi province.

It was late at night. She had traveled seven hours to meet me. When I walked in the room, I saw this beautiful little girl playing with her nanny. Twice in my life I've felt like I've won the lottery—both when I first saw each of my children. Maggie was three and a half years old.

I had a doll for her that her cousin had picked out and sent along. She ran over, grabbed the doll out of my hand, and ran back to her nanny. I had some cookies that the facilitator recommended I give to her. She came over to try some of the snacks. We had to take some pictures that night, as she was coming into my custody prior to the adoption. After all of the paperwork was completed, we got into the car.

Maggie was very scared and cried "Wo yao Nana" (I want Nana). We took her back to the hotel room. I gave her a bath, which she liked, and I dressed her in her new pajamas. She stopped crying for the bath, and she stopped again to admire herself in the mirror in her new red feetie pajamas.

We didn't sleep well that first night. Since she was too big for a crib, she slept with me. She woke up frequently. I had heard that kids of all nationalities like to play "peek a boo" with a scarf. I hid my face under the scarf and said, "Where's Momma?" Then I took the scarf off of my face to say, "There she is!" Pretty soon, Maggie was playing along and had learned the English words.

Maggie and I adjusted to each other quickly. I had brought along some baby books and a picture book of her family which her cousins had made for her. She studied the pictures and was very affectionate with everyone who had their picture in the book once she had returned home. In the baby books were pictures of body parts. I told her the English words, and within a week she was pointing to her nose and eyes and using the English words.

After a week, we left Nanchang for Guangzhou. We would do the final paperwork for her U.S. visa there. Maggie and I went on walks in the morning. I showed her the Chinese ladies dancing for exercise along the river, hoping she would drink in some of her culture. We also played on the playground in Guangzhou. By now she was only crying about once a day, and she and I were getting closer. She loved the breakfast at the hotel, and could tell me "Wo yao/bu yao" (I want or I don't want), every bit of food. She liked to carry her own plate and to climb into the high chair by herself.

We shopped a lot while we were there, picking out clothes for her and presents to take back home. We did some sightseeing in Guangzhou, going to the temple and to Three Goat Park, as well as some other sights in the city.

Finally, it was time to go to the embassy. We got on a bus with a lot of other families, and we all filed into a large room. The ambassador's assistant came out and gave us a talk. We all raised our hands and pledged that we were truthful to the process. Then one by one our facilitators came back to us with our passports and visas. We left for the States the next morning.

Maggie had a good flight. Thanks to all of my business travel, we had business class seats, so she had her own small TV (with Baby Einstein). We had packed pajamas, and she slept for a good part of the flight. On the last leg of the trip, she got a little testy, but then, so was I. We were greeted at the airport by Maggie's new family who had smiles, balloons, and gifts.

Maggie has had issues adjusting, but she has learned English quickly. She is intelligent and is well along for a child who had not seen a letter of the alphabet until about eighteen months ago.

I won't say that being a single mother with two small children is easy. I admit there are days that I wonder what I have gotten myself into. Then something happens—usually one of my girls says something cute—and I remember why I wanted to be a parent to begin with. Being a parent is a rewarding experience that I wouldn't trade for anything.

Sharon Pohly

Henry and Jack and a Mommy Makes Three

God could not be everywhere, and therefore he created mothers

—Jewish proverb

    What must it be like to belong to no one? I wanted to begin the story of my grandson's adoption with a sentence that would capture your attention and move you, so that you want every acquaintance to read this book. I want you to understand the struggle these precious babies face. Though *this* story has a happy ending, let us not forget all the little ones still waiting for a home.

    My daughter, a single woman, had decided to adopt a child from foster care. It had been two years of paper work, classes, and inspections. In the meantime she busied herself preparing a room for her new arrival. As the months passed she began to give up hope. The pre-adoptive meetings she attended were filled with people who had been waiting up to four years. With so many children needing a home, how could this be?

    One day a call came for her at work from DSS (Department of Social Services). It was a Friday. Unfortunately she never received the message. It wasn't until she arrived home that she learned there was a child available.

It was an emergency situation and he needed to be placed immediately. She tried to call DSS several times that evening but was unable to get any information. On the last attempt she was told that the boy, whose name was Henry had been placed. Her heart was breaking. It was a long weekend of wondering what had happened to Henry. Monday finally arrived and Henry's worker called her. It had only been a temporary placement, and she would be getting him.

On November 21, 2006 an eighteen-month-old boy lay on my daughter's floor hysterical and crying. We knelt next to him and tried to comfort him and we cried too. He had been abandoned at birth, and had been exposed to drugs and alcohol before his birth. He had received no prenatal care. Now at eighteen months he was in his third home. He had been placed in a foster home at four days old. It was the only home he had ever known for eighteen months and now in less than a week he had been moved two times. Here he was, with sadness I can't imagine, wondering where he was and who we were. He had come with some toys and luckily my daughter chose the right one. It was a little vacuum that played the "clean up" song from Barney. For forty-five minutes she played that song over and over. Finally he stopped crying and got up and went over to his toys—the only things that were familiar to him. There was no way to let him know there would never be another move; he was home.

We were given very little personal information about him—only the simplest things you would tell a sitter. Does he talk? What does he like to eat? How does he like to go to bed? Does he have a favorite song? The list could go on. Those of us who are parents know that these simple preferences are security to our children. How sad that nothing was known about his life to help him with this transition. We didn't know when the last time was he had eaten. My daughter fixed him spaghetti. He ate like he hadn't eaten for weeks. By then he had been there for two hours and the entire family had gathered to welcome him. He still preferred to have everyone just sit nearby but not actually hold him. We had to go slowly to reassure him and make sure he could learn to trust just one more time. It was love at first sight for all of us, but especially for my daughter. At the inception of this pre-adoptive process my daughter had said she would only take a child that was adoption-ready. On several occasions over the next few days we were assured he was. But then, less than a week after his arrival we found out the biological parents' rights had not been terminated. The prior social worker had failed to file the proper papers and follow through on her duties. Now it was like starting from scratch.

In addition we now knew the original foster family had filed to have their home reopened and to regain custody of Henry. A feeling of panic consumed us all. We were Mommy, Grammy, and Pop-Pop to Henry. He had aunts, uncles, and cousins. Henry was ours and we were prepared to do whatever it took to make it legal. It was Thanksgiving weekend. Henry was our object of affection and what we were thankful for that year. In a few short days he had become a part of our family. Our feelings were no different than if he had been born to us.

He was sick when he arrived and so the first week was spent getting medical attention. He had only been seen at clinics and we were applying to private physicians so he would have a physician who knew him. It was difficult with little medical history.

Considering all he had been through and how he was unable to understand what was happening, he began to adjust. We could finally hold and hug him and we did so as often as he would allow.

Sleeping was a big problem. Since we weren't familiar with his routine, we let him guide us. For the first few months he cried himself to sleep while we held and rocked him. He would wake up in a panic—hysterical, crying, and not fully awake. While he slept, someone was always within a few feet of him, ready to hold him close and assure him he was never alone.

As weeks passed my daughter continued to press for an adoption date. Finally, good news came, or so we thought. A court hearing was to take place on January 24 that would terminate the rights of the parents. We called the court-appointed attorney for Henry the following day to find out the results of the hearing. We were informed the hearing never took place. My daughter was also told at this time not to concern herself with the prior foster family's petition to reopen their foster home because it would not happen. The hearing for the prior foster family took place in June. Not only had their house been reopened, but they were now filing a petition to have Henry returned. On July 18 the biological father was released from prison and on that day he filed to block the termination of his rights.

The panic we had felt Thanksgiving Day was nothing in comparison to what we were feeling at this time. It took us until September to get a private attorney to agree to meet with us. One after the other had turned us down. Time and again we were told it was hopeless and nothing could be done. They wished us good luck. Henry's state-appointed attorney had been little help as we tried to find out our options. We will always be grateful for the attorney who did meet with us. She gave us the key to help ourselves. My daughter downloaded Consent to Adopt forms off of the internet. The only information we had on the biological father was his name, last known address, and place of employment. We spoke to his last employer and with the information he gave us, we transferred our search to a specific location. For three days we hit the streets. Up and down, day and night, we walked, talking to anyone who would talk to us. Finally we found him. After convincing him we were not with the police or any other government agency he talked to us. By the fourth day we had his forms signed and in hand. He led us to the biological mother and a few days later she also signed. We also found out the biological mother was pregnant with her sixth child. It would be the same situation—no prenatal care and exposure to drugs and alcohol. My daughter was in no position to care for an infant, but he was a sibling and would be born alone and abandoned. To her the choice was obvious.

We knew that the papers that had been signed would not be acceptable to DSS. Our ace was that the courts would have to hear our side now. The biological parent's signatures could not be dismissed. My daughter called Henry's worker to tell him what she had done. I know he was secretly proud of her. He is a caring man himself. This was his job, and so he brought us the proper required consent forms. Once again we hit the streets. By the next day the papers were signed by both parents. Finally we thought we were on our way. Henry's lawyer was furious with my daughter for taking matters into her own hands. But she was Henry's mommy and she would have walked through fire to save her child. Henry's attorney could have easily given those forms to my daughter, but she never gave her the option. How could we not utilize all means to give Henry a permanent home?

On October 26, 2007 a call came from the biological mother to my daughter. She had just delivered Jack, Henry's brother. The biological mother told my daughter she had signed over all of her rights at the hospital. For all intents and purposes my daughter would have all of the rights of mother to new baby Jack. After the call I sat with Henry while my daughter went to see her new son. The hospital would not abide by the biological mother's request. She was only able to peer at Jack through the glass, just like any other stranger. He was so small, just a little over four pounds. He was going through withdrawal. Here she was, ready to hold and comfort him, and she could do nothing. Every day after the first visit she called but was never allowed to see him. Attempts to reach someone at DSS who could straighten out this mess proved futile. On November 1, she reached someone at DSS. She inquired about Jack's condition and when she could see him. She was told he had been placed in foster care. How could that be? She was his mommy and he was with strangers.

Angels hover over my grandsons. People move in and out of our lives, but I have begun to realize it is not without purpose. On November 5, my daughter located Jack. He was still hospitalized and going through withdrawal. He was also having trouble learning to suck. He had been transferred to a pediatric hospital. My sister has a friend who works there. My daughter also works with a woman whose daughter works there. They indeed verified he was there. One of them had just finished doing an evaluation on him. With these contacts, my daughter was finally able to be with her baby. Jack was thirteen days old. For the first time the only mother he would ever know was there to hold and comfort him. He was sick but now he had a family who could love him to wellness. Jack came home on November 7, 2007.

When a baby is born he is given a temporary worker and so was Jack's case. My daughter immediately called Jack's worker for Consent to Adopt forms. He was not aware of this option. Henry's worker gave us the forms for Jack. By this time we had contact numbers for the biological parents. The forms were signed and delivered. Jack would be one of the few abandoned children who was lucky enough to only know one home. He has been loved since birth and he has always had a family.

At first Henry was not quite sure why Jack was there. Henry had been the center of the universe for a year. Since then he has adjusted; some days are better than others. Jack is seven months old now. Henry is three years old. On February 20, 2008 Henry was legally adopted. The entire clan was present for the adoption.

Henry is extremely bright. I say that not as a grandparent with delusions. He amazes me every day. His spatial ability is astounding. He is above the curve on comprehension. It was suggested that he see a speech therapist by DSS. His appointment was a few months ago. He whizzed through all of the developmental tasks. They said he could come in and teach; he passed with flying colors. He recently did a vocabulary study at Johns Hopkins University. He is bright. Jack is also bright and alert—at seven months he is on par with his peers. He is one of the nosiest babies I have ever seen. Sometimes he can barely drink his bottle, afraid he will miss something. He has been alert since his arrival and he loves to laugh. He recognizes our voices and puts his hands out to be held. Jack also completed a study at JHU concerning an infant's ability to comprehend numbers. He was one of the few babies that didn't cry, but I am not sure of his math abilities. Considering everything these boys went through in utero, they astound me every day. I only mention these things because I don't want you to be afraid to adopt babies who are born exposed to drugs and alcohol.

It is so difficult and time-consuming to adopt a child in my area. I have been working on options to ease the laws. I want to impress upon the judges how important it is to terminate the rights of children born in such dire circumstances. The faster they are placed in a permanent, loving home the better. Don't give up. Do whatever it takes. You can fight the system. We did it.

A devoted Grandmother

Nicole

Life and Measurement

Life can not be measured
By things we do or say
Everyone will make mistakes
4,000,000 times a day
Not only children make mistakes
Adults can make them too
And their mistakes are leveled also
Not only by a few.

Daniel Kastello (age 8)

    Nicole was born January 21, 1989. In March 1989, her father, Melwin Cowen, brought her to me. He said her mother wasn't caring for the baby. He said her birth mother would just give Nicole a bottle and put her to bed. When I first got Nicole she could do nothing. She would just lay there—no laughing, no smiling, and no crying. Absolutely nothing! After about a week of me constantly talking to her and playing with her, trying to get some kind of emotion from her, Nicole finally smiled. After that she started to show emotions. Through a lot of therapy and lots of love, Nicole began to interact by cooing and playing. She was able to do all the things a normal baby would do.

Through all this, Nicole's father tried to stay in her life, however when Nicole was four years old I applied for adoption. It had been difficult to care for her, as every time I would take her to the doctor's I would have no legal rights and would constantly need the father's consent and permission. A lot of the time he was nowhere to be found.

At the adoption hearing as I sat waiting for my turn, the most bizarre thing happened! I sat next to the cutest little girl and her mother. I began to play with the girl. When the judge called for the lady next to me. She stood up and said, "I am Nicole's mom." I was shocked. I had never seen her before. Nicole's biological mom continued by saying that she had a drug habit, but was doing better and wanted Nicole back. I was stunned! The judge put off the adoption for another month to give the birth mother time to get her life together. That month was the longest month ever. I wondered daily if Nicole, whom I loved and cherished and had nurtured, would be mine or not.

Finally on our court date, Nicole's mother gave up all her parental rights as did her father. I was so relieved.

There have been times when it has been difficult as there has been no financial support form her birth father and the state has not been much help either. All in all, we are very blessed that we have never gone without. Life was hard at times but with the God's help we never suffered.

I love Nicole with all my heart just like my other children. She is my daughter, my gift from God.

Gail Slade

When All the No's Finally Become Yes!

While we try to teach our children all about life,
Our children teach us what life is all about.

Even as a small child, I knew that children were going to be an important factor in my life. I was only nine when I started a preschool in my neighborhood, bringing all the kids together and teaching them things like numbers, letters, and songs. As an adult, I had two biological children and cared for most of my nieces and nephews. I ran an in-home day care for years and coached softball and boy's soccer as well. I was the Cub Scout leader and one of the first parents who volunteered to help at school when help was needed. Kids seemed to be an integral part of who I was.

God had placed it in my heart as a child and I had always known somehow, someday, that I was going to end up raising children that I didn't give birth to. I had seen these faceless children in dreams throughout the years. I had never encountered anyone who had adopted, much less fostered children, or I am sure I would have been involved years before I was. I had known people were adopting infants here and overseas, but I was well aware that the cost for such an adoption was in the tens of thousands of dollars. A cost that was well out of my ballpark at the time.

About ten years ago, I talked with a friend about foster care, which I knew existed, but it was then I found out that there were a lot of children who ended up *not* being able to go home to their parents. I had never really thought about that. I guess I had always assumed that they all went home, or . . . well, I never really gave that much thought before. These kids became available to be adopted.

It wasn't until I met my current husband, James, that the idea of adoption really became a serious thought. When a person or couple first begins to consider adoption as a way to "grow" their family, the entire process can feel very scary and overwhelming. The internet is full of thousands and thousands of websites on the topic of adoption and sifting through them can be a daunting task. Plus, well-meaning family and friends can bombard you with horror stories of "adoptions gone wrong" and misconceptions. With all of that in mind, I had begun researching adoption, knowing nothing about domestic adoption except for the little I had been told years ago. I happened to stumble onto a site called Faces of Adoption (now known as www.AdoptUsKids.org). There were so many children here in the United States that needed parents. Children of all ages were posted, and there were listings for sibling groups and children who had special needs. I was astounded! How had I not known about these children all of these years? I knew right then that I wanted to adopt a child from foster care. Upon reading further, I realized that it wasn't like in the olden days, when you just went to an orphanage and picked one out and took them home. There was a process.

When James came home from work that day, I showed it to him, and he reminded me that he had grown up in foster care himself. If he and his brothers had not been returned to his mother, he too could have ended up either being adopted or aging out. Most times when he and his brothers were in care, they were split up for reasons unexplained to them. Some homes were fantastic to them and in others some of them had been abused. The more we talked, the more we decided how important it was that siblings stay together when they can't go back home. It was then that we knew God had a plan for us, one he had begun orchestrating long before we knew it—or each other. We then decided we wanted to adopt a sibling group out of the foster care system. It was hard enough for children to be split from their parents, family, and friends. We wanted them to always have one another.

I called a friend who I learned had adopted a child this way, and asked her for her agency's information. She led me to a wonderful agency. The director, Paula, has been a blessing to our family. She was so kind and full of information. We had been cautious and leery of some stranger delving into our lives, but Paula made it comfortable and even enjoyable for us. She completed our home study, which consisted of each of us writing an autobiography, taking over thirty hours of classes spread out over the course of a month of Saturdays, and getting criminal and child abuse clearances and FBI fingerprinting done—not to mention all the numerous home visits and interviews. Once she had all of this in order, she wrote our home study for caseworkers to read and the searching process began.

We had decided that we would adopt two, three, or possibly four children. Since James was on the road as a truck driver most of the time, I spent many days searching through the photo-listing sites on the internet and asking Paula to send out our study for children of interest. A photo-listing is a brief paragraph or two of children available for adoption as well as a picture of them. It seemed like forever that we were sending it out, and we began to wonder what was wrong with us that we weren't being chosen. We were a great family, and yet no one was selecting us. It became a little discouraging, but we knew we could not give up. Our children were out there somewhere. We knew eventually we would get selected.

One day, while searching a site, I came across a listing for a sibling group of seven children from California. I told James about them, and he laughed and said, "They sound great, go ahead and send our study. It isn't like we are going to be chosen anyway." A few months went by and we continued to send out our study for other children of interest. One day, Paula called to announce that we had better sit down. Well, imagine our shock and elation when she announced that we *were* chosen for the seven of them! I called everyone we knew, including our two other kids, Angie and Joe, who were as excited as we were. Most people thought we were out of our minds. That didn't matter to us. These were going to be our children, and we would become one big family.

When I informed my parents and siblings about what we were about to undertake, they all thought we were crazy. My brother tried very hard to talk me out of doing it. That was, until they actually met the children face to face. Then the reality of it sank in. These were just kids, not unlike any other kids, who wanted to be loved and accepted. Now my family would give their lives for any of them.

The hardest part was waiting for all the paperwork to get done, so that the children could move to Pennsylvania. It was during this time that we went out to California twice to visit with the children. The first time we went for two weeks in August. We only got to see the two oldest girls because someone had dropped the ball and didn't get the judge to sign the order for the other children to visit with us. The other children were in a different foster home. Meeting the girls face to face after only seeing them in pictures was amazing. They had already been given a photo album from us, so they were looking forward to seeing us too. We took to them immediately and they clung to us. The two girls didn't understand why they didn't get to leave with us when we left the first time, and leaving them behind was the hardest thing to do.

The second trip was supposed to be for another two weeks, and did include visiting all seven children, but it ended up being for four weeks due to additional court hearings about abuses by their foster parents coming to light. Can you imagine spending a month in a two-bedroom hotel room with seven children you just met? Well, we did, and we all made the best of it. The children were not used to being with each other and were all very combative with each other. They all hit, pinched, kicked, bit, shoved, smacked, and dug at each other to get their way. We had them all broken of that before leaving the hotel at the end of the month. We simply gave them one rule: "Keep your hands and feet to yourself." They have asked if they can go back to California. When we asked why, they said they want to go back to the hotel to swim.

During the second trip we had issues with court hearings, abusive foster parents, and termination of rights all while we were there. But in the end, the reward was so worth the battle! They came home with us that trip. We did offer their biological mother and grandparents a chance to see the children before we left, so they had the chance to say good-bye and give their family closure and so our children could emotionally move on. They took us up on that offer, and told us that meant a lot to them. I am still in touch through email and phone calls with their grandmothers.

It was a little chaotic and hectic when they first arrived, and it took a few weeks for everyone to adjust to each other as the kids hadn't been living with each other for years. The youngest didn't even really know the oldest. But we had plenty of help from our adult children, whom James and I are very proud of for their efforts and accomplishments. Most children would have been jealous and resentful, but Angie and Joe have embraced their roles with the kids with love and commitment. Angie and

Joe have been awesome role models, as well as being some of the kids' favorite toys. The kids were happy to be back together with each other, and to be a part of a real family. How awesome it is for Angie or Joe to walk in the door and have seven younger siblings shouting their name with glee and running into each other trying to get the next hug.

Our children have all adjusted beautifully, and have been flourishing in their new lives. Support from our church family has been one of the strongest threads holding our children and family together throughout this transition. For that, James and I are very thankful. Our family is now one big happy family who all support each other.

We attend each other's events. Most of our community has seen the Lands Clan on the bleachers at the baseball fields cheering for each other. Other families enjoy being around our family. They say there is nothing like hearing all of our family cheering on one of our kids—a family big enough to be a built in cheering section. Remember when we all secretly wished we could be one of the Brady Bunch, the Walton kids, or the Partridge Family? Remember when being a part of a big family was the normal way of life? When families were known for their values, morals, and traditions? Our family has been blessed with this opportunity, and we embrace it with open arms and Christian faith.

Our story doesn't end there. The children recently asked James and me, "When can we get some more kids?" They said we are such a good mom and dad and that there are other kids out there who need us. So . . . we are in the process of doing it all again. This time our family, friends, and community are all behind us. Well, most of them anyway. And our eyes are open wider as to what to expect, but the excitement is still the same. Each child is a blessing to our lives.

In closing, I ask that you please pray for the children who go to bed every night, praying to never be abused or neglected again and hoping that a family comes forward to take them home forever and show them that God hears and answers their prayers. Pray that they can they be adopted into an earthly family, but, more important, that they become adopted into the kingdom of heaven.

Sharai McConnell Lands

Bringing Our Children Home

*Her children arise up, and call her blessed;
her husband also, and he praiseth her.*
Proverbs 31:28

When my husband Justin and I married, one of our goals was to have a very large family. We each had lots of siblings, biological and adopted. Both of us had experienced firsthand the happiness that is found in a big, united family. We also knew what a valuable learning laboratory a home can become when many individuals work each day to learn to love one another and to serve one another. Such an environment can maximize a child's potential to be well-adjusted and able to handle every situation encountered in society. We could not think of a better way to provide our hoped-for children with a great foundation for life.

In the first years of marriage we happily welcomed five beautiful daughters, thinking that we were well on our way to the ten or twelve children we had prayed for.

No more children came. Miscarriage after heartbreaking miscarriage dashed our hopes of giving our children the big-family experience we had dreamed of. Even as we enjoyed our little daughters and recognized the profound blessing of having them, we were troubled by an empty, sad, "someone is missing" feeling.

Adding to our anxiousness to have more children were vivid dreams through the years. They were more than dreams. In them we were shown children who needed us! In one there was a pretty, ladylike little girl, a dark-haired, stalwart little boy, and a tiny baby boy whom I carried in my arms. Another dream featured a blond baby boy, who looked like he was about nine months old. There were several dreams of a little black haired, dark-complexioned girl. First I saw her as a baby, in the next dream she was a three-year-old, then in another she looked like she was about five. These dreams were real. So was the experience one night when I was awakened by a child saying "Mama" in my left ear. I quickly opened my eyes, but was no one there. I hurried to check the girls to find which one needed me. They were all fast asleep. These children we saw and heard were real, and I could not erase them from my mind or from my heart.

The above paragraphs cannot describe the depth of our feelings. Anyone who has desired children without being able to have them knows what we felt. The years of disappointment, anguish, and physical and emotional pain defy description. Those who have never had this desire would not understand it no matter how precisely it was described. Those who have lived it need no explanation.

Finally we decided to try adoption. After all, the black-haired girl who kept coming in dreams didn't look like she was produced from our gene pool. We read about state agencies begging for adoptive parents. We determined that we would seek to adopt children who might not have opportunity to ever have a family—sibling groups or children with disabilities. We attended orientation meetings and had a preliminary interview with the appropriate state agency representative. We felt relieved that we were finally moving forward.

I will never forget the second appointment we had with the state agency individual. He sat across the desk from us and calmly told us that we were not good candidates for adoption because we had too many children. He also cited the age difference between my husband and myself and appalled us by suggesting that if we divorced I would be acceptable as a potential adoptive mother. How do people like him get jobs that can mess up innocent lives?

We went out to the car and just sat in the parking lot and cried. Then we prayed and told the Lord that we were going to officially give up every dream and every effort to build a bigger family. We had tried and tried and nothing had worked. We affirmed our willingness to love and to care for any and all children he wanted to send to our family—but if we were to have any more, he would have to bring them because seven years of trying had convinced us that there was nothing more we could do.

A month to the day later, the phone rang, and in one conversation my niece Shirley changed our lives. She had served as a missionary in Russia and had done volunteer work in orphanages. Through a long series of events, she had recently encountered an American couple who over the years had managed to adopt six children from Russia. She had told them about us, and they had offered to share their experiences if we wanted to call and talk to them.

What did we have to lose? We called Barton and Julie Jones and they told us exactly how they had completed the adoptions. They discussed agencies and facilitators and explained laws and requirements. As the conversation ended they said something that played over and over in my mind. "If you decide to adopt we will do everything in our power to help. We would do *anything* to help more children get out of orphanages!"

My husband and I discussed what we had learned about Russian adoption several times that evening. We also spoke of information we had previously gathered about adoption from other countries. Trying domestic adoption had been a disaster. Could our missing children be in another country?

Early the next morning I was working in the kitchen. My husband came in and without any preamble stated, "I feel very strongly that we are to adopt children from the city of Vladivostok."

This was not like Justin. Normally things of import were mulled over for days and carefully weighed and considered. Here was an absolute pronouncement that would bring about earth-shaking change for our family. I was shocked but excited. Justin was an inspired man, and I knew that he had learned the Lord's will for our family.

The next year was the hardest one we had ever known. Justin was working on a sculpture commission with an impossible but necessary deadline. At the same time we were learning how complicated international adoption is. Our lives were a roller coaster ride of emotional highs and plunging, heart-stopping lows as week by week we scrambled to meet all the legal requirements so that we could bring our children home. Barton and Julie Jones were true to their word. We called every time things were too confusing or discouraging, and they always knew how to help.

After our official dossier was approved, we were given basic information on several children and told that we were to make a preliminary choice based on the faxed information. Prayer and fasting brought direction as we agonized over the decision. We called Victor Artamonov, our facilitator in Vladivostok, and told him of the children we felt would be right for our family. There was a startled silence after we told him that we wanted to adopt Alexander, Aleksei, and Victoria. He said "This is rather miraculous. All the time we have adoptions where parents choose children who look like them, but you have not seen pictures of any of the children whose information I sent you. The brothers you have chosen look like Justin's picture, and Victoria looks like LaRee."

Finally pictures of the children came in the slow, slow mail. I remember standing ready to pounce on the poor mailman who had been mercilessly cross-examined each day as we waited for the package to come. I frantically ripped open the packet of pictures he handed me and gasped to see photographs of a dainty, ladylike little girl, a dark haired, stalwart boy and his adorable little brother. They had been younger in that long-ago dream, but I recognized them immediately.

Months later, after countless prayers, hundreds of miracles, and harder work than we had ever dreamed of, Justin and I flew to the other side of the world. During the long flights we listened to tapes of Russian survival phrases that Shirley had prepared for us. At least we would be able to offer our new children food and water, and tell them when it was time to go to bed.

We arrived in the Russian Far East at the frozen end of January 2000. Even my Michigan-reared husband was astounded at the intensity of the cold. There, for the first time, we met Victor, the coordinator who had moved mountains for us in Russia. The year of constant communication made us already feel close to this great man who had found our children for us.

Victor knew how anxious we were to meet the children, and took us to the orphanage even before we went to the hotel. In the dream the children I saw had been healthy and vibrant. As they came shuffling into our presence in the orphanage, we saw that they were thin and ill-clothed. They were also very cold in spite of the layers of miss-matched, worn clothing they had on. Justin sat them on a couch and spread his overcoat across them, and they grinned with excitement that their new father was looking after them.

I couldn't look at them enough! I didn't want to scare them with the smothering hugs and kisses I longed to give. It took real restraint to be friendly without getting overly emotional. How could they know how many years we had been longing for them?

This new daughter was tiny! Nearly nine years old, she fit nicely into size six clothing. She had dark brown hair, beautifully shaped brown eyes, and an adorable little turned up nose. Her official name was now Victoria Rose Fairbanks, but the Russian nickname Vica (Veeka) suited the mischievous twinkle in her eye. Just as the dream had shown, she was ladylike and feminine. Vica had been in an orphanage since her biological mother's death six years before.

Alexander Avard Fairbanks was known by the Russian nickname Sasha. He hated it and told us that he wanted to be called Alex. Like Vica he had brown eyes and brown hair. He was athletic, outgoing, and excited about airplanes—he couldn't wait to fly on one to America.

Alex was the biological brother of Aleksei (pronounced Alek*say*), who became our Seth Aleksei Fairbanks. Seven-year-old Alex was protector to Seth in the rough world of orphanage life, and after they met Vica he protected her also.

Seth at four-and-a-half was a tiny fellow who kept up a never-ending flow of talk. His constant monolog was a running commentary on life; some in Russian, some in baby talk. Much of his conversation had to do with suggestions that more chocolate would make life better.

The boys had been in the care of their great-grandmother, and were put in an orphanage after her death. They later told us that they never had enough to eat while in the orphanage, but it was a lot more than their poor grandmother had been able to give them.

We have heard many harsh things said about orphanages, but our experience left us with feelings of gratitude for good people doing the best they can. Russian orphanages suffer because of lack of resources. The orphanage officials and workers we dealt with were nearly all kind, caring, self-sacrificing people who worked like heroes in a tragically difficult situation. The orphanages were old but they were clean. During our many days of visiting the children we developed great admiration for the many workers who selflessly wear out their lives caring for hundreds of helpless children.

The judge officiating in the adoption had required that we come long before the court date so that we would have an opportunity to get acquainted with the children. Each day we would make our way through the snow and ice to get to the orphanage. Victor, his wife Lilia, or one of their two daughters would guide us through the public transportation system and lead us down the frozen roads to visit the children. They stayed there to help interpret, and we often had other visitors during the visiting hours as well. Social workers came to assess our rapport with the children. Student social workers came to learn how to observe our interaction. Each day we longed for the time we could take the children and just start being a family.

Back in the hotel each day Justin and I had a lot of time to be lonely. We missed the children who were stuck in the orphanage. We missed our five daughters who were staying with my sister's family while we were off in the wilds of Russia. Each day brought hope that when the hotel's business office was open there would be an email from the ones we missed so much at home. Weekends were terrible because the business office was closed till Monday and we couldn't hear how the children were or send accounts of the adventures we had each day in Vladivostok.

Finally the court date came, and we nervously prayed our way through the hearing. We were asked many questions about our home situation and desires for more children. The home study, medical forms, income statements, and other legal documents were carefully reviewed. It was obvious that the judge and the other court officers had real concern for the children and wanted to determine as far as was possible that they would be entrusted to people who genuinely intended to be good parents. We rejoiced as the judge announced her approval of the adoption.

There were more days of visiting at the orphanage while the ten-day legal waiting period wore itself out. Victor and Lilia were working fast to prepare all the documents necessary for the children to receive visas from the United States embassy in Moscow. Finally, the evening before we were to leave Vladivostok for Moscow, we were allowed to bring the children from the orphanage and be together in our room at the Hotel Versailles.

The next hours were a comedy. We tried to converse with memorized Russian survival phrases combined with some wild and crazy charades. We wondered if the famished children would ever stop eating. It was incredible to see how they crammed food in and swallowed it almost without taking time to chew. Anything they did not finish was immediately stashed in pockets or the little backpacks we had given them. It was obvious that they had great uncertainty about when or if there would be more food.

The next morning we finished packing and fit ourselves, our new children, and all our luggage into Victor's car. Parting with Victor, Lilia, and their twin daughters Helen and Kate was like leaving family. They had served us so faithfully and given help in ways we would never be able to repay.

Finally it was time to board the plane. All three children were excited, but Alex was *ready*. He had lived for this moment. He grabbed my hand and hurried me along for this much-anticipated moment of actually getting on an airplane.

It seemed so good to board our flight to Prague that evening, where we spent what was left of the night in a hotel. We were hundreds of miles closer to our children waiting at home! The next morning we gratefully boarded the Czech plane that would take us to America.

As the long hours of the trans-Atlantic flight dragged by, the children went through all the stages of travel fatigue know to man. After they had grown tired of all the in-flight amusements we had packed, a flight attendant helpfully gave the children some balloons. As soon as they blew them up and started playing with them she hurried over to tell me that the children were misbehaving. Go figure.

About the time we approached the East Coast of the United States all three children blessedly fell asleep. This gave me a little time to think about the reunion that would come five hours after we boarded the flight to Arizona. We were so lonesome for the daughters waiting there with our kind family members who had cared for them in our absence. Nothing less important than the adoption could ever have induced us to leave them, and finally the long separation was nearly over! For the first time in our lives we would have all our children together.

While the children slept, the past year of incredibly complex adoption work flowed through my memory. I thought of times so hard that I had been ready to give up, and how Justin's steady, faithful counsel had pulled me together and kept me working through the exhausting details and requirements. I thought of friends and family who had encouraged and helped us beyond anything we ever could have asked. I especially remembered "coincidences," which were really tender mercies from a loving Heavenly Father who always knew exactly what kind of miracle we needed next.

The flight monitor showed that we were very close to the Newark airport where we would board our last flight. I reached over a sleeping child to lift the window blind and see if anything besides ocean was visible on our side of the plane.

Just at that moment, right in our line of sight I saw a small island in the harbor below. In amazement I recognized Lady Liberty standing with her torch aloft to welcome our children to their new country. I reached across the aisle to grip Justin's hand and together we gazed at our tiny, rag-tag, sleep-drenched, travel-weary immigrants and wept with gratitude that a thousand miracles had brought them home!

LaRee Fairbanks

Laree and Justin Fairbanks adopted a total of twelve children from Russia before he passed away. They have seventeen children altogether.

I Had Dreamed of Being a Mother as Long as I Can Remember

Beloved, if God so loved us, we ought also to love one another.
1 John 4:11

When Jerry and I finally met at the end of 2000, I had pretty much given up on all my dreams of ever mothering, homeschooling, and staying at home. I had been in the corporate world for twenty years and really enjoyed it; I decided that if "Mr. Right" should come into my life at this point, the miracle of marriage would overcompensate for any dreams of parenting.

It was nearly "love at first sight," with both Jerry and I. We both sensed a supernatural force drawing our union. On our journey of courtship, we spoke often of "investing in the next generation," and helping the homeless and the aging. Both having strong leadership backgrounds working and volunteering with non-profit groups, we enjoyed dreaming of how our past would unite in a common new vision. We began to formulate ways to "give our life away" and make it count for the big picture. We felt investing in kids' lives was imperative. It all started when a couple who had been living in Haiti for five years approached us over dinner, asking us to consider working alongside their mission staff. We took the offer seriously. It was completely in line with our values and prayers. We felt working with the orphans, poor, and needy in Haiti was exactly what we should do.

Our world shifted dramatically due to a couple of books I picked up randomly at a drug store. Dave Pelzer's "The Child Called It" was on the New York #1 best-seller's list, and "The Lost Boy: How Foster Care Changed My Life" caught my eye. I gave these books to my speed reading husband one Sunday after church. He didn't move from the couch until he was finished with the first book and began the second. In the middle of the second book, I could see something taking place in his heart. Nearly finished with the book, Jerry exclaimed, "This is it! This is really it!" I had no idea what he was talking about, but I was all ears. Jerry was excited to share with me his vision of helping the orphans "in our own backyard" rather than across the world. Having grown up in a split family and living much of my formative years in children's homes and in foster care myself, I didn't need convincing. I called about foster care classes immediately, and we were enrolled within the month. The next six months we played the waiting game, jumping through the myriad of hoops. We became licensed foster parents in the fall of 2002.

In my own "perfect world" that I created (the figment of my imagination) I wanted to help as many children that we could. I was separated from my brother most of the time when I was younger, though my sister and I stayed together and developed a strong bond that continues to this day. It was my hope to keep siblings together and help them be reunified with their parents (just like what happened in my life) as quickly as possible.

As Jerry and I began this journey as foster parents, we wanted to share a home and love with a few children, thinking it would be a temporary ministry opportunity, until our son (and only child), Chris, graduated from high school. The first call we had from the state was to provide respite over the long Labor Day weekend for a sibling group of three boys. Six weeks later these same three brothers moved into our home forever. They were up for adoption, having been in the system off and mostly on for over six years. At fourteen, ten, and eight, (Tyler, Cody, and Joseph—respectively) the likelihood of them being able to stay together in an adoptive home was improbable. We weren't sure we wanted to adopt, but we were sure we didn't want these three brothers thrown to "the system," continually bouncing—or separated (as their other three older siblings had been).

A year later we did take the adoption plunge. More than a few tears and prayers were offered until we decided that these were *our* boys and we would be their parents *forever*. The decision to adopt has affected everything in our lives, including my decision to quit my corporate job to stay home when we began fostering.

A year after our adoptions were final, we felt a desire for "two more girls." We began to pray and call the state placement coordinator, paint the room, and prepare our hearts and lives to receive more. When we received the call about our daughter Jewel, who was not quite two and a half, we felt it was exactly what we wanted for our brood of testosterone. It would take another six months of visits with her parents and agreeing to an open adoption before we would finally adopt her nearly one and a half years later. At four years old now, she is very well-adjusted and finds her place in this world of boys and men very comfortably. She is a rare "Jewel among jewels," loved by all.

I understood the incredible need to provide a safe, "therapeutic" family to these children who have lived such traumatic, stressful lives. After two years of watching the kids struggle in their classes to maintain grades, we decided to homeschool. We now have time to go to the weekly counseling, and various doctors' and special-needs' appointments that inevitably surface with our "failure to thrive" kids.

Only four years have gone by and we look around at our thriving home that is producing character, values, and ingenuity. Those who were lagging behind are now producing grades above level (Cody's state tests were astounding this past year—averaging 4.6 grades above grade level—this from one who was facing his second "failed" grade in elementary school). Wow! We are thrilled to be in this bonding process with such amazing kids and we are privileged to be called "Dad" and "Mom" . . . a title we do not take lightly.

Jina Ezell

You're Never Too Old to Make a Difference!

When you put faith, hope and love together, you can Raise positive kids in a negative world.

—Zig Ziglar

I grew up in a rather dysfunctional home. My mother was abusive to me and my brother and she was a very controlling person. My father was in and out of the home during my early years as my mother was extremely controlling with him, also, and filed for divorce on many occasions. As odd as it sounds, even though he was missing in action at times, my father was my rock and my stability. Along with him, my maternal grandmother was as protective of me as she could be and I give her and my father much credit for protecting my brother and myself.

I cannot tell you exactly at what age I made the decision, but at some point early on in my life I decided I would never be like my mother and that someday I would adopt children and take them away from any abuse they were suffering at the hands of their parents. In fact, I told my grandmother there were three things that I was going to do in life. I had a fascination with Native American culture thus I was going to marry and

"Indian," I was also going to own a red convertible, and I was going to adopt unwanted children. My first husband was in fact part Cherokee; I did eventually own the red convertible; and I have now, in the latter years of my life, adopted children. The children, of course, are the most important, challenging, and fulfilling part of my life to this point and I cannot imagine anything better.

I began attending college after my second oldest was born, and I fell in love with the field of psychology. It was a struggle to go to school, work full time, and parent two young boys, especially later as a single parent. My college career ended up on hold for nearly thirteen years, and it wasn't until my youngest son was born that I was able to return to school. Up to that time I had held various retail and factory jobs but once I was able to do an internship and had the college experience under my belt, I was able to begin working in the field of mental handicaps/mental retardation with both adults and children, and there has been no going back to any other type of work.

When my youngest son was only seven or eight he was diagnosed with bi-polar disorder, and my going thru a divorce from his father only exacerbated his issues. We began counseling and the long journey to his adulthood, and it was a long and exhausting journey. It was during that journey that I considered using my experience with children through employment and with my own biological children to assist other kids by doing foster care. And, quite honestly, being a single parent, it was a way for me to bring home some extra income and have time at home with my own children. It seemed like a win-win situation for me and my family and in fact, it turned out to be just that.

I began doing therapeutic foster care, which I know now is one of the toughest for beginners, and have not looked back since. After a year or so of doing this I gained a reputation with the agency of being the mom who took the hard cases and did well with children with more severe issues. I felt as if I had finally found myself and my niche. It was very rewarding and satisfying. Then a little boy came into our lives and was there for quite a time. More than anything, I wanted to adopt this child. Due to the system, which I consider quite faulty, this was not to happen. I became very much frustrated and disheartened with the agency I was with and when he left my home I decided to take a break and concentrate on my own children who were teens at the time. It wasn't until I took that break that I had realized how consuming this little guy I was caring for had been. Not until then did I realize that I could no longer do foster care. I no longer had the heart to give the children back when the time came to do so.

Around three years passed and my youngest turned eighteen. I began checking into foster care again. I really wanted to adopt but was convinced by the agency that being in the foster-to-adopt program was the way for me to go. I was older and single and, not knowing what I do now, was easily convinced that my chances of adopting were limited to this particular setting. Again, I found myself in the position of doing foster care and getting the hard cases. I just wasn't happy doing this, as my goal was to adopt and raise children as my own. I missed having children in the house, and it wasn't just empty-nest syndrome. I simply wanted more children and wanted them to be permanent members of the family. I wanted to be sure they would be there for holidays and that the bonds they were making with the extended family would continue and not have to be broken at some point in time.

Quite honestly, there was selfishness in adopting, also. I felt defeated every time I had to return a child to the same situation that put them into foster care to begin with. While I think I knew that they would take at least some small part of the love and learning they had in my home, I also felt like a lot of that was going by the wayside. I just felt as if I was devoting all this time, love, and attention and that in the long run, it wasn't making that much of a difference because I wasn't able to "save" the child from the very system that was supposed to help him, not put him back into harm's way.

By this point in time, I had been with an agency for over a year and had absolutely no leads on children to adopt, so I began my search for an agency that would in fact help me meet that goal. I felt as though I had wasted yet another year in my search for my new children. Being older, I felt like time was running out for me. I was convinced that the older I became, the less likely anyone would look at me as a permanent resource for any child. I was very blessed to find my current adoption worker as she is unbelievable. She is so positive, and her only agenda is to see that the children out there in the system find forever homes.

With her my searches became more intense and within six months of signing on with her, my first two boys were placed with me. The oldest had a form of autism and his younger brother was deemed "normal." I was totally elated, knowing that my family was now expanding and that when these children came into my home, there were there to stay. I worried that something would go wrong right up to the time I brought them home, but as time went on, I realized they were my children and here to stay. It was shortly after this that my worker called and asked me if I would consider doing foster care for a boy who had been disrupted from two pre-adoptive homes through no fault of his own. I was hesitant, not just because I had just brought my two sons home, but his diagnosis of MR/autism concerned me as I was not sure I would be able to handle it all. But as it turns out, I am now in the final process of adopting him also. All three of my children, even with all of their special issues, are great kids and bring love and laughter into the home. They love unconditionally and appreciate all that is done for them and given to them. We have had some rough patches with adjusting, which are to be expected, but it is as if they have always been a part of my family. I couldn't love them more if they were my biological children; they are just my kids.

I have received many comments concerning my desire to adopt at my age. Mostly I have been asked, "Why?" The only answer I can truly and honestly give is, "It is just what I do." I have been told I am nuts by some—that these should be the years when I am sitting back and enjoying life after having raised my biological children. I don't quite understand this type of comment. I am very much enjoying raising my sons, and they have brought so much love and "life" back into my life. What could be better than a houseful of loving kids—a house that sometimes is in a state of positive chaos, but always busy and full of energy? What better to keep me young? Mostly I have been asked, in a kind way, what made me take "that kind" of child, which I assume refers to their issues. I don't really see "issues," I just see my boys. They are individuals, just like any other kids. They have their strengths and weaknesses, just like anyone else.

It isn't likely that any of my sons will grow up to be NFL players or go to Harvard or Yale. In fact, two of the three may never at any point in time be able to live totally independently. It may well be that none of them are able to marry and have children. All of that is okay with me and not an issue at all. In fact, I sometimes joke that the advantages are that I don't have to go through teaching them to drive (a very nerve-racking experience if you ask me!). I don't have to worry that I will someday get a 2 AM phone call that there has been a car accident. I don't know that I will miss the "normal" teen age rebellion and behaviors! I doubt very much that my boys will ever be in a position to be introduced to drugs or alcohol and have this as an issue, and so with all of that in mind, what else could a mother ask for?

Maybe it's because I am older or because of my extensive background in the field, but I, in my older years, am relishing the simpler things in life along with my boys. I think I had forgotten some of that somewhere along the line. Simple accomplishments excite them as well as me. Recently there was a meeting concerning my older boy and someone said that in all the years they had known him this was the first time they were able to maintain eye contact with him and actually stay on a set subject during a conversation with him. She was thrilled to even be able to carry on a conversation of some substance with him. It took work on both our parts to accomplish this. I spent months of feeling a little guilty that I would refuse to respond to him unless he looked at me while speaking, but it needed to be done and it did in fact result in a very positive outcome. I was very proud of him and that accomplishment, and when I was able to explain to him in terms that he could understand, he was very proud of himself too.

My other son had been in an inclusive classroom in his previous placement, and I pushed for a mainstream class for him. He has absolutely blossomed this year in school and he is very proud of that. How could a mother expect more or ask for more than children who love to learn, who push themselves to excel, and who are so very proud of their goals being met?

I am in no way the perfect parent—if there is such a thing. True, my skills in parenting have grown over the years, and I believe my patience is much better than it has ever been, but my kids have played a roll in all of that. In all, I truly believe that they have given much more to my life than I have to theirs.

I continue to search for additional children to add to our family. I would really like to adopt children who have some type of physical handicap because I feel I could contribute greatly to their lives and they to ours. Further, I have already considered what I will do when my search is over and my family complete; I have decided to become an advocate for those in the process of adopting and assist them in the process in any way possible. I have spent years now on the computer, searching for children and researching the system, and feel if I can put that time to use to assist other children in finding permanent homes I will be accomplishing much. This has all become such a wonderful, rewarding, and valuable learning and growing experience for everyone involved and I would encourage anyone who has the means and heart to give a child a home to consider doing it. You won't be sorry you did.

    Chris

Ask, and it shall be given you; seek and ye shall find;
knock and it shall be opened unto you:
For every one that asketh receiveth;
and he that seeketh findeth;
and to him that knocketh it
shall be opened
St Matthew 7:7-8